Walking through Time with Jesus

DENNIS DICKEY

WESTBOW
PRESS®
A DIVISION OF THOMAS NELSON
& ZONDERVAN

WestBow Press books may be ordered through booksellers or by contacting:

WestBow Press
A Division of Thomas Nelson & Zondervan
1663 Liberty Drive
Bloomington, IN 47403
www.westbowpress.com
844-714-3454

ISBN: 978-1-6642-8865-2 (sc)
ISBN: 978-1-6642-8866-9 (hc)
ISBN: 978-1-6642-8867-6 (e)

Library of Congress Control Number: 2023900338

Print information available on the last page.

WestBow Press rev. date: 01/25/2023

I dedicate this book to my wife, Wende Sue Dickey. She is an excellent editor and proofreader. In her wisdom, she declined to edit and proofread this book, believing that fifty years of marriage was more important than correcting the errors in this book.

Photos By Celeste provided the author photo and wrote the author biography. If you need photos, she is excellent! She is also my daughter.

My sister Lorene Dickey drew the original artwork for the cover. She took the idea in my head and turned it into a work of art.

My friend Gordon Dasher read my manuscript and offered suggestions and corrections. He has my sincere thanks.

I must also include Tom Stocum, who kept saying, "How is that book coming?" Well, Tom, here it is!

My Purpose for Writing This Book

There are many books discussing the visions of John. Is another book needed? Can what I have to say add clarity or just more confusion? Why has someone else not already written this book? These are some of the questions that have gone through my mind as I have taught Bible classes that focused on the book of Revelation.

I have always tried to use the scripture to explain scripture. I believe God has said what He intended. I also believe that God is consistent in the words He inspires. Every scripture God has inspired is based on the same truths. Each scripture will complement every scripture. Together they form a picture of God and truth. The best way to understand what God is saying is to listen to what God is saying. Many times, we read or listen to the words, but we only hear what concerns us at the moment. Our underlying thoughts color the words of God with our desires. Even when those desires are noble, they can still distort the pure message of God.

As I set out to study the book of Revelation, I made a strong effort to understand the message God intended. Using the words in the revelation of Jesus and those words as found in other scriptures, I endeavored to leave out popular commentary and only see what God had given. Following this pattern, I reached the conclusions written in this book. Looking at teaching materials and commentaries about John's visions, I did not find any that matched what I had discovered from the verses themselves. I write this book to share with you the lessons I have discovered from my studies.

In this simple book, I attempt to share my thoughts to help others find a message that will help them understand God's message of salvation.

A humble servant,
Dennis Dickey

Contents

Introduction xi

Chapter 1   The Visions Begin 1
Chapter 2   The Message to the Churches 5
Chapter 3   More Letters to Churches 14
Chapter 4   A Visit to the Throne of God 20
Chapter 5   A Plan for Creation 26
Chapter 6   Christ Breaks the Seals, Creation Begins 29
Chapter 7   There Is a Pause in Heaven 32
Chapter 8   Breaking the Last Seal 35
Chapter 9   The Adversary Moves to Creation 41
Chapter 10   God Introduces His Law 46
Chapter 11   The Law Serves Its Purpose 48
Chapter 12   The Conception and Birth of Jesus 52
Chapter 13   Satan Makes War on Christians 56
Chapter 14   The Beginning of the Last Days 60
Chapter 15   A Scene in Heaven 66
Chapter 16   Pouring Out God's Wrath 69
Chapter 17   The World Is Judged 76
Chapter 18   Worldliness Is Doomed 81
Chapter 19   Heaven Rejoices 84
Chapter 20   The Fate of Satan 88
Chapter 21   A New Place to Live 93
Chapter 22   A Picture of the Heaven to Come 96

Appendix 99
Index 103

Introduction

What is prophecy? The last book of the Bible, Revelation, is often said to be the only book of prophecy in the New Testament. Is it? Let's look at what the Bible says about prophecy

Much of God's interaction with men, either written or spoken, is done through spokesmen called prophets. Using these prophets, God teaches men proper behavior and tells the consequences for not obeying God's teachings. Men watched their futures unfold in compliance with God's statements. They assumed that the prophet had foretold the future and did not accept that God had made the future. This caused prophets to become known as seers, predictors of the future. Kings would seek prophets to ask the outcome of battles before they were fought. Prophecy came to mean predicting the future, and prophets were expected to foretell the future.

The biblical definition of prophecy is speaking for God. "Then the LORD said to Moses, 'See, I make you as God to Pharaoh, and your brother Aaron shall be your prophet'" (Exodus 7:1). God has often used His prophets to warn His people of His future actions—not a prediction but a revealing of His will and the results. The same, you say. No, God does not predict the future. He creates the future.

The last book of the New Testament is sometimes labeled a book of prophecy. It is, but it is not the only book of prophecy in the New Testament. Jesus refers to Himself as a prophet in the Gospels. "And they took offense at Him. But Jesus said to them, 'A prophet is not without honor except in his hometown and in his own household'" (Matthew 13:57). He also speaks about things to come, most notably His coming crucifixion and the destruction of Jerusalem. His presence and words are not for the purpose of foretelling but for calling men to repentance and faith. Each of the Bible books was written by men "speaking for God," and each could be labeled prophecy. They all contain references to the future history of men.

Because the words "shortly come to pass" are written at the beginning of John's book, many people see this writing to be completely a prediction of the future. Looking for a match between current events and the visions of this book and trying to predict the future will cause the reader to miss the true purpose of John's writing.

There have already been several historical events that could be said to match the "prophecies" of this book. Because of the human nature, events in history tend to repeat themselves. "That which has been is that which will be, And that which has been done is that which will be done. So there is nothing new under the sun" (Ecclesiastes 1:9). Because that is true, events at different points in time have been matched to the same visions in John's book. This will continue to occur until the end of time. Do not miss the message of John's visions because you are looking for predictions of what will become human history.

The Revealing of Jesus Christ

The last book of the Bible begins with the words "The revelation of Jesus Christ" (1:1). This is not a book about future history but a book about Jesus and his role in creation—future, past, and present (during the time of the visions). Jesus was and will be present throughout the history of man and will continue His presence through the future of man. Jesus calls Himself "the Alpha and the Omega," the beginning and the end.

The story of Jesus does not begin in a manger in Bethlehem or in Nazareth within the virgin womb of Mary. The existence of Jesus begins before time and will continue when time has ended. When the world was made, Jesus was there. "Let Us make man in Our image" (Genesis 1:26). When Adam hid in the bushes, Jesus was there. When the first rainbow was painted across the sky, Jesus was there. When Moses saw the burning bush, Jesus was there. When the Israelites returned from captivity, Jesus was there. When Rome was just a small city, Jesus was there. All things were made by Him, through Him, and for Him.

---- CHAPTER 1 ----

THE VISIONS BEGIN

Who wrote this book? What is the setting of the book's origin? What did the author and God intend us to learn from the book? These are all questions we need to keep in mind as we explore the message of Revelation.

John Introduces Himself: Revelation 1:1–3

John, the last living apostle, introduces himself as a brother and a fellow sufferer for the cause of Christ. He does not elevate himself above the people to whom he is writing. The church has been established and is beginning to feel the effects of the forces of evil. Physical persecution has scattered the church throughout the world. All the other apostles have been killed for their faith. John himself has been exiled to the island of Patmos because of this persecution. Satan is spreading the lie that Jesus is not coming back. Deceivers are teaching that He has not risen from the dead. False teaching is becoming prevalent, and the believers are beginning to doubt their faith.

These visions are given to John to share with his fellow believers, both those living and those to come, as an assurance that the Gospel message of resurrection is true and lasting. He is commanded to write and share what he sees and hears with seven established churches in Asia. What he writes has been preserved and is shared as part of the inspired Bible today. The visions in this writing are a blessing to all those who hear and believe.

A Vision of the Christ: Revelation 1:1–4

John's visions begin with the resurrected and ascended Jesus watching over His church. John hears a loud voice "like the sound of a trumpet," clear and precise (1:12). Trumpets are used to make announcements, give battle signals, and celebrate victories. This is a commanding voice, one to be obeyed and not questioned. The voice carries words of instruction. "Write in a book what you see, and send it to the seven churches." John receives detailed instructions about his visions. This is God's message, not John's.

Jesus Appears to John: Revelation 1:5–8

John's description of his vision is very specific, highlighting the unearthly quality of what he sees. The objects in this vision are common to John's period of history. A man in a robe, lampstands, stars, and a sword. Yet they are described in a way to enhance their glory. The man is more than a man; His feet shine, and His hair is whiter than wool. His eyes are like flame, and even His voice is different, sounding like many waters. The man in the vision is more than mortal man and is indeed Jesus Himself. The sword coming out of His mouth cuts both ways, both praising and condemning, separating good from evil by His words. Jesus speaks truth that shows every lie as a falsehood. All these objects are highlighted to emphasize their glory. This is not just a lonely man dreaming of what he knows but a message from the glory of heaven! The simplicity and vividness of this vision are typical of all the visions in John's book. There is no mention of any floor supporting the lampstands or of any background scenery. Only the objects needed to express the message of the vision are described.

One "like a son of man" is described with precise detail—clothing, hair, eyes, feet, and even the sound of His voice. He is the center focus of this vision. He is the Alpha and the Omega, overshadowing all else. It is His voice that explains the vision and draws the eyes to each detail as He speaks. A voice that is both frightening and unforgettable.

Jesus deals first with John's fear, just as He did while present on earth. (Matthew 14:27 says, "It is I: do not be afraid.") John will remember the night when Jesus came walking on the sea and used much the same words. The words are similar, but this time, Jesus gives a more complete identity. He speaks of His eternal existence and His resurrection. He also references the authority He has been given over death and hades. He gives John instructions on what to write. The visions will be of things that exist and things that will come to exist. Then, surrounded by the other objects, He explains the meaning of this vision.

Jesus among the Churches: Revelation 1:9–20

Jesus explains the stars are the angels of the seven churches. The word *angel* is often said to mean a messenger from heaven (1:20). These angels have each been assigned as the messenger to a specific church, each with a specific message. The message can be specific for each church because Jesus is walking among them and knows them.

The lampstands are churches, groups of people who believe in the resurrected Jesus and follow His teachings. The lampstands are made of gold, giving them high value. They are crafted and special, showing care and love was used in their making. The purpose of lampstands is to hold and share the light. Light is often used as a symbol of the Word of God. Jesus called His followers the light of the world. "You are the light of the world. A city set on a hill cannot be hidden" (Matthew 5:14). A major function of His church is to display the light of God's glory found in the message of the Gospel. "Let your light shine before men in such a way that they may see your good works, and glorify your Father who is in heaven" (Matthew 5:16).

Jesus's explanations of these visual symbols will remain consistent throughout John's visions. Stars will be angels, and lampstands will be people holding up the light of God's Word. If stars are explained as angels in this vision, then stars will be angels in later visions. In chapter 12, John writes of a war in heaven between Michael and Satan that involves "stars." These "stars" are not from this world but from heaven. Because Jesus says these stars are angels, we accept that the heavenly beings at war in the vision described in chapter 12 are also angels. The angels here appear in the hand of Jesus and are under His command.

Jesus is walking among the churches that have sprung up in His name according to the teaching of His apostles. His churches are not left alone to stumble their way through the future. He is present, both observing and guiding the churches. He gives specific commands aimed at specific problems, commands that show knowledge of each church and of the individuals that collectively are the churches. He stands among the lampstands. This puts Him in their presence where He can watch over them and reach them if they need tending. Jesus has not abandoned His people to their own resources but walks among them with an angel assigned to each congregation to see to their needs.

CHAPTER 2

THE MESSAGE TO THE CHURCHES

As we read about the messages to the seven churches, we ask ourselves, "Why these churches? Why a different message to each church?" If the message is to a certain church, why do I need to read the message?

The Letters to the Churches: Revelation 2:2–3:22

Each of these seven churches is a congregation composed of Jews and Gentiles, people from all nations. These churches are located on major trade routes and will influence many cities and shape the message of Christ as it moves through the world. Each church has a unique setting that creates a trial of their faith related to their unique circumstances. The test of faith for each church can be a lesson on how we respond when our faith is tested in a similar way.

Our temptations of the flesh may appear different because of circumstances, but every believer will overcome each temptation by faith in Jesus. These seven churches have already been named (Revelation 1:10), and are all churches where Jews and Gentiles worship together.

Each congregation is different, and each congregation receives instruction and encouragement specific to them. Each message reveals an intimate knowledge of every member in the congregation. With a voice like the sound of many waters, Jesus continues speaking, giving John words to write to each congregation. The first message is to Ephesus.

Ephesus: Revelation 2:1–7

When the apostle Paul came to Ephesus, it was a flourishing port city. More than seven centuries old, the city was perhaps second only to Rome in its influence and wealth. In the city was a temple to the goddess Artemis. More than five centuries old, this temple rivaled the Parthenon in size. The worship of Artemis was a large part of the city's economy.

Paul, after speaking in the synagogue at Ephesus, journeyed on. He left behind Priscilla and Aquila to nurture the believers there. Later, Apollos arrived in the city and began to preach Jesus, teaching only the baptism of John. He was taken aside and instructed "more fully" by Priscilla and Aquila. "And he began to speak out boldly in the synagogue. But when Priscilla and Aquila heard him, they took him aside and explained to him the way of God more accurately" (Acts 18:26). When Paul returned to Ephesus, he found disciples knowing only the baptism of John. After Paul taught them about Jesus, they were again baptized, this time in the name of Jesus.

Paul stayed for three months, teaching in the synagogue. When he began to meet with opposition from the silversmiths, he was taken before Gallio by the Jews. To avoid further conflict with the Jews, he moved with the believers from the synagogue to a nearby school and continued teaching for two years. Word spread throughout Asia of his success in teaching and of the many miracles he performed. Paul's success began to affect the local economy, and his opponents started a riot that had to be settled by the local government. "About that time there occurred no small disturbance concerning the Way" (Acts 19:23). After this was settled, Paul left and continued traveling and spreading the teachings of Jesus.

Jesus begins His message to this same church located in Ephesus by stating His position among the churches. He is walking among them—not off somewhere sitting on a throne like an earthly king who is unaware of the daily lives of each of his subjects. The words "I know" tell of a direct knowledge of their deeds. Not "I was told" or "I have heard" but a knowledge that shows that He is personally aware of them and has not abandoned them. As we read the words written to the church at Ephesus, we remember Jesus saying He would be with His people. "For where two or three have gathered together in My name, I am there in their midst" (Matthew 18:20).

His first words to the Ephesians are words of praise expressing the things that they are doing well. He praises their endurance and persistent desire for the truth. He speaks of their strong stand against false teachers and strength of purpose, not growing weary but pushing forward in the face of tribulation. He then speaks of their weakness, saying they have left their first love. Their allegiance is no longer to Him. They now serve something or someone else. Perhaps the church or the people, or some man-made doctrine.

Jesus demands our complete loyalty. Serving the church or a religion or even good works may feel like we are being loyal to Jesus, but it is not. Remember the words of the apostle Paul. "Whatever you do in word or deed, do all in the name of the Lord Jesus, giving thanks through Him to God the Father" (Colossians 3:17).

Jesus offers them an opportunity to lift themselves back up. To do this, they only need to turn (repent) and do the things that they did in the beginning. Serving Jesus is not hard. The yoke of Jesus is easy and His burden is light. "For My yoke is easy and My burden is light" (Matthew 11:30). They have repented before. There is no excuse for not returning to the proper path. Being warned and not obeying will have its consequences. Jesus says He will remove them from His presence and all the blessings His presence provides. He leaves them with a word of praise placing them alongside Himself in their hatred of the Nicolaitans. If they are together in this way, why not in all else?

"He who has an ear to hear let him hear what the Spirit says to the churches." This statement tells us today that this is a timeless message. It is written here to the church at Ephesus but is a message of hope and salvation for anyone who listens and heeds the teaching of Jesus. There is a reward for anyone obeying the instruction of Jesus—ready access to the tree of life and a place with God the Father!

Smyrna: Revelation 2:8–11

With an economy spurred by Roman trade, Smyrna was a prosperous port city challenging Ephesus and Pergamum for the title "First City of Asia." Located forty miles from Ephesus, Smyrna was at the head of a major trade road. There was a strong gathering of saints in Smyrna composed of both Jews and Gentiles. There was also a strong Jewish opposition to the congregation located there.

Jesus begins His message to the church at Smyrna by reminding them of His authority. He has always been and will continue forever to be the Alpha and the Omega, the first and the last as described in chapter 1. He is the firstborn of the church. The founder, leader, and owner of His church that he bought with His blood. His sacrificial death is proof of His love, and His triumph over death is proof of His power and His ability to take care of His own. What Jesus promises, He can and will accomplish!

Speaking as the resurrected Christ, He reminds them that He too faced tribulation and that He overcame both tribulation and death. Having lived on earth in human flesh, Jesus is no stranger to the pain they are facing. He knows what He is asking of them and the strength they need. He knows their lack of material things but also knows they have treasure already stored in heaven. He urges them to look beyond the physical and focus on Him.

Their tribulation is well known to Jesus. He can name the false Jews they face and calls them collectively a "synagogue of Satan," placing them directly in opposition to Himself. They are your enemy, and they are allied with my enemy; we will oppose them together.

The devil will seem to be succeeding, but he will not succeed. This message to Smyrna is personal. Jesus tells them some of them will be thrown into prison. To paraphrase, Jesus reminds them: I was also a prisoner and I was killed. You face the opposition of the world; I overcame the world. You face death; I have conquered death. I have not abandoned you. The time of this suffering will be short. Hold fast, and you will triumph.

The message says ten days. Numbers and times in the visions given to John are symbolic in the same way that the images are symbolic. Ten is a number that often means completeness. Your period of testing is set and limited to what Jesus will allow. When the time of testing is finished, it will end.

Jesus calls this a test. He is allowing Smyrna to be tested to strengthen their faith and their confidence. Jesus does not have to test us to know the level of our faith, but we need the test and adversity to strengthen our faith and to give us proven character and hope. "And not only this, but we also exult in our tribulations, knowing that tribulation brings about perseverance; and perseverance, proven character; and proven character, hope; and hope does not disappoint, because the love of God has been poured out within our hearts through the Holy Spirit who was given to us" (Romans 5:3–5).

Jesus already has their reward ready, a crown of life. A crown they will wear after leaving this world. Death, whether it comes sooner or later, is their door to eternal life even as it is ours. Tribulation may only end in a physical death, but endurance will result in life eternal. That is the promise of Jesus.

This epistle to Smyrna ends with a promise to everyone who overcomes the trials they face because of their faith. Those who overcome will not face the second death. "Then death and Hades were thrown into the lake of fire. This is the second death, the lake of fire" (Revelation 20:14). Death is not God's desire for man. He warned Adam in the garden about the possibility of death if Adam would not listen. Here He warns about the fate of those who will not listen and heed His warnings to the churches. "Then He will also say to those on His left, 'Depart from Me, accursed ones, into the eternal fire which has been prepared for the devil and his angels'" (Matthew 25:41).

"He who has an ear let him hear what the Spirit says to the churches." Jesus admonishes the saints at Smyrna to listen and heed the message He has sent them. Jesus also makes it clear that the different messages are not just for the churches to which they are first delivered but to everyone who has ears and is willing to listen.

Pergamum: Revelation 2:12–17

Pergamum was once a thriving metropolis to rival Athens with a library second only to the one at Alexandra. The earliest known history of this city dates to 300 BC. A small city of only 532 acres, Pergamum was built on a plateau. Access was made possible by three connecting terraces.

Under Greek rule, the city flourished. The people attempted to remake their city into a copy of Athens. The city grew more than four times in size and at one time became an independent kingdom.

The description of Jesus as the one with the two-edged sword emphasizes that truth cuts both ways. Truth is truth, spoken or unspoken; truth does not change. A person's character does not change because it is hidden. In fact, true character cannot be hidden from our Lord. God sees into the heart and judges by intention as well as action. Our deeds are a combination of both intention and action. Jesus sees our deeds in their completeness.

After identifying the source of the message, the message continues with praise for the deeds and faith of the saints in Pergamum. They have a strong faith and have remained faithful even while some among them were being killed for their faith. Holding fast to a belief in the existence of Jesus does not always result in proper doctrine or behavior. Remember James says the devils believe and tremble. Jesus does not reject His people because of weakness. Rather, He sends them a messenger to admonish poor behavior and encourage improvement. God and Jesus want us to be our best and have worked tirelessly through the ages to help us be our best.

The wheat and the tares grow together. God wants it this way because no one on earth can separate the two. Paul at one time would have been purged from those called God's servants. Every saint was at one time a sinner. We see the outside, but God sees the heart. Good hearts can be overlooked and those with evil hearts can be missed by human eyes. But God sees all.

I know where Satan's throne is. I know where Satan dwells. The message is plain. Jesus is saying "I will deal with Satan, look to yourselves". Each person there is accountable to God for their own deeds and beliefs. Some are leaning toward the sins of Balaam and others toward the philosophy of the Nicolaitans. This is a message like the one God spoke to Cain before he slew his brother. "Then the LORD said to Cain, 'Why are you angry? And why has your countenance fallen? If you do well, will not your countenance be lifted up? And if you do not do well, sin is crouching at the door; and its desire is for you, but you must master it'" (Genesis 4:6–7). As long as we are alive, we can repent and change our relationship with God.

The story of Balaam is told in the book of Numbers. Balaam has become a symbol of those who claim to follow God yet seek the pleasures of the world at the same time. Following the way of Balaam is trying to walk a thin line between service to God and serving oneself. Jesus makes it clear that this is impossible. "No one can serve two masters; for either he will hate the one and love the other, or he will be devoted to one and despise the other. You cannot serve God and wealth" (Matthew 6:24). God wants our complete and absolute loyalty.

Scholars do not agree concerning the philosophy of the Nicolaitans. Nicolaus was a common name during this time. Also, during this time, there were several deviations from the Gospel. The message is not about this particular false teaching but that they had yielded to a false teaching. If it is not the pure Gospel, it is a false gospel. The message here is to remain true to the truth. Jesus will not tolerate variations in His teaching. Those that change His teaching will be attacked by the two-edged sword—the truth. The desire of our Lord is that those who have strayed will repent and return to the straight and narrow way.

Each of the messages to the churches ends the same way: "listen to Me." Jesus expects His people to heed the message He has sent them. After His admonition to heed His words, Jesus speaks of hidden manna. Manna was the bread that sustained the Hebrews during their forty years of wandering. Now Jesus is the bread that comes down from heaven and gives life and strength to His people. This manna is only for those who are true to His teachings. Those who do not follow the truth cannot accept His life-giving words.

Furthermore, just as Simon was given the name Peter to mark his service to our heavenly king, we too will be given a new name. This name will be carved into stone enduring for all ages. Followers of Christ become new people transformed by His grace and forgiveness. The stone is white because it is washed and clean. Just as a child of God is washed clean in baptism and begins a new life with a new name.

Thyatira: Revelation 2:18–29

Thyatira was a Roman trade city known for dyeing cloth and for its indigo trade. Lydia, an early convert, sometimes called the first convert in Europe, was from the city of Thyatira. "A woman named Lydia, from the city of Thyatira, a seller of purple fabrics, a worshiper of God, was listening; and the Lord opened her heart to respond to the things spoken by Paul" (Acts 16:14). The city was of mixed races and religions. The strongest religion of Thyatira was the worship of Apollo.

Trade in the city was organized by guilds. The two most powerful were the coppersmiths and the dyers. Guilds functioned much like our modern corporations. They were able to own property and enter contracts and had a strong influence on the local economy. The guilds with their secrecy and rules would present the saints with hard choices. Do they follow the guild rules and prosper or the teaching of a risen Savior and gain life eternal? Should they give their loyalty to Jesus in private and to the guild in public or serve Jesus with their whole lives?

The image of Christ given at the beginning of this message describes His eyes and feet. Eyes to see and feet to travel. Not normal eyes but eyes of flames. Eyes able to see that which could be hidden from ordinary eyes. The eyes that are like a flame of fire that see into every heart and mind. Nothing is hidden from His sight. All is revealed so Jesus can render to each of us, the just and the unjust, just what we need and merit. Do not deceive yourself. Christ will make no mistake in His judgment. Feet made of bronze that would not tire or be deterred from their journey. When Jesus says, "I see," that means that nothing is hidden, and when He says, "I will come," we can be certain that nothing will stand in His way.

Jesus is telling the church; He knows what they have done and what they are doing. He also knows that they are doing more than they have done in the past. But He also know what they have left undone. They also tolerate evil they should reject. "I know your deeds, and your love and faith and service and perseverance, and that your deeds of late are greater than at first" (Revelation 2:19). Jesus again says, "I know." We cannot hide from His "eyes of fire." Jesus sees everything. He knows our every motive. He knows the source of evil in Thyatira.

That evil is described as a woman named Jezebel. In the first book of Kings, Jezebel was the wife of Ahab and incited him to do evil. "Surely there was no one like Ahab who sold himself to do evil in the sight of the Lord, because Jezebel his wife incited him" (1 Kings 21:25). Encouraged by Jezebel, Ahab committed murder, stole land, and worshiped idols. He persecuted the prophets and caused God's people to worship Idols. Just like

Ahab's wife, this woman of Thyatira was leading God's people in the paths of unrighteousness. We must be careful to only follow those who follow Christ. "Be imitators of me, just as I also am of Christ" (1 Corinthians 11:1). Who we choose to follow can determine our eternal abode.

God does not want anyone to perish but wants everyone to repent and survive. "The Lord is not slow about His promise, as some count slowness, but is patient toward you, not wishing for any to perish but for all to come to repentance" (2 Peter 3:9). This Jezebel was no exception; she was given time to repent but refused. Because of her evil ways and her refusal to repent, God promises an end to her evil ways. Her life will become a torment and those who are drawn away from God (into idolatry) will also face death. The destruction of her influence and her followers will confirm to the world that the church, the body of Christ, is under His control and His protection.

Some of the disciples at Thyatira did not fall under Jezebel's influence and were not led astray. They will not be burdened. Jesus did not come into this world and establish His church for it to fail. Our burdens are often of our own making. These faithful disciples at Thyatira are encouraged to hold fast to what they have and not lose faith or courage. They are promised a place in the kingdom of God with authority and the morning star. This message ends with the admonition to listen. Listening to God is not just hearing the words but includes hearing the words, knowing who spoke the words, and making the words a part of your life. Just as they were encouraged to listen to Jesus, so are we. Only by paying close attention to the words of Christ will we escape the danger of sin in our lives.

CHAPTER 3

MORE LETTERS
TO CHURCHES

What is special about the message sent to each church? Is there anything in each message that is relevant today? What does Jesus mean when He encourages us to "hear"?

Sardis: Revelation 3:1–6

On the banks of the Pactolus River, Sardis was at one time the capital of the kingdom of Lydia. When gold was discovered in the golden sands of the river, Sardis became one of the first places where coins were minted from gold. Because of their wealth, the people of Sardis felt secure in their existence. They were living the good life but were neglecting their souls. The wealth of the city gave a false sense of safety and security. Their wealth made it hard for them to reject the pleasures of this world and be satisfied with the spiritual riches of Jesus. Perhaps because they felt that beginning the path of following Christ was enough, they failed to carry through with a transformed life. Trusting in their wealth instead of trusting in Christ, they did not grow in their faith but remained immature and unfruitful in their work for God.

The message from Jesus is a command to complete their conversion. The rich, young ruler in the Gospels was told "one thing you lack." "When Jesus heard this, He said to him, 'One thing you still lack; sell all that you possess and distribute it to the poor, and you shall have treasure in heaven; and come, follow Me'" (Luke 18:22). He did not need to put his trust and delight in worldly wealth; rather, he needed to turn loose of the world and trust in God. He was given the next step to becoming a creature of the spirit and not a servant of the flesh. He was told put your trust and loyalty in Christ and not in the wealth of this world. This is also where the people of Sardis failed. They still clung to their trust in their riches and had not fully committed to God. They are given an opportunity to repent and are warned of the consequences if they do not.

There are a few people in Sardis that Jesus praises. He knows the record of each individual and judges each man according to his own deeds. We are not saved or condemned by the congregation we attend, but we can be influenced by the company we keep. "Do not be deceived: 'Bad company corrupts good morals'" (1 Corinthians 15:33). They are encouraged and reminded of the reward promised. Their sins will be covered with white garments and they will be introduced to the Lord God Most High. If they confess Jesus on earth, He will confess them in heaven before God, His Father. "Therefore everyone who confesses Me before men, I will also confess him before My Father who is in heaven. But whoever denies Me before men, I will also deny him before My Father who is in heaven" (Matthew 10:32–33). Once again, the message ends with an admonition to listen to the message from the Spirit. Let Him that has an ear (everyone who will listen) hear what the Spirit says to the churches.

Philadelphia: Revelation 3:7–13

Founded in 189 BC, the city of Philadelphia sat at the base of a mountain along the trade route between Sardis and Laodicea. The land near the city was suitable for producing grapes and at one time produced a favored wine of the Roman empire. The city was sometimes called little Athens because of the large number of temples and public buildings.

Philadelphia was nearly destroyed in AD 17 by an earthquake. Because of its importance to Roman trade, the city was quickly rebuilt.

Jesus is described to this church as holy, true, and having God-given authority. He has the power to open and shut, and that power is given to no one else. His authority from God is confirmed by the promises made to David through the prophets. "The Lord has sworn to David A truth from which He will not turn back: 'Of the fruit of your body I will set upon your throne. If your sons will keep My covenant And My testimony which I will teach them, Their sons also shall sit upon your throne forever'" (Psalm 132:11). The unquestioned authority of Jesus gives Him the power to keep open the door just as He promises. The power of their faith in Jesus has enabled them to keep the teachings of Jesus. Because they have been steadfast and faithful, Jesus rewards them with this open door. Those who do not deny Jesus the Son will be recognized before God the Father. "Therefore everyone who confesses Me before men, I will also confess him before My Father who is in heaven. But whoever denies Me before men, I will also deny him before My Father who is in heaven" (Matthew 10:32–33). They are being assured that their faith is recognized and will be rewarded.

Some scholars believe this to be the door of the kingdom; others consider this to be a door of opportunity. Doors are a way out or a way in. A door that cannot be shut sounds like an opportunity to leave where you are and go to someplace better. Perhaps this door symbolizes a way of escape from the torment of the Jews in their city. That escape could take any number of forms, including death. Death for a Christian is another step in the journey home to be with God in a place without tears and tribulation.

The synagogue of Satan is denounced by Jesus for professing faith and having none. It is, at best, a voice of denial to the Christian faith and, at worst, active physical persecution of the faithful saints in this city. Jesus tells the faithful in Philadelphia that the synagogue will come and bow down at their feet. Since we have no recorded history of the event and since the hist1848ory we do have makes that unlikely in this world, this is probably an event that takes place in the next world. The image of the unfaithful Jews bowing down to the faithful saints must be in the future.

As bad as things are for these saints who are commended for their perseverance, there are worse things to come. Jesus promises to spare them this future tribulation. He calls it a testing of the whole world. Every generation of Christians faces trials or testing. This testing can range from direct violence to the temptations of easy living. Following God requires faith and trust in times of trouble and in times of plenty. "Two things I asked of You, Do not refuse me before I die: Keep deception and lies far from me, Give me neither poverty nor riches; Feed me with the food that is my portion that I not be full and deny You and say, 'Who is the LORD?' Or that I not be in want and steal, And profane the name of my God" (Proverbs 30:7–9).

Just as Jesus recognizes His faithful, He also sees those who have an opportunity to serve Him but fail to acknowledge His authority and truth. Those who are faithful will be as much a part of God's dwelling as the pillars that hold up the temple. The faithful who remain faithful no matter what will belong to God and everyone will know they belong to God. Their fellowship with God will be known as surely as if they had God's name written on their foreheads for all to see. Once again, this message is for all who will listen and heed its promises and warnings.

Laodicea: Revelation 3:14–22

Located on the Lycus River, Laodicea sat at a crossroads of Roman trade routes. The major source of income for the city was trading in textiles. They were famous for a black wool and for their tunics. Trade also included marble, cattle, and grain. Because of the available minerals located near Laodicea, they also became known for their eye salve. A large Jewish population from Babylon was settled there by Antiochus III the Great in 200 BC. This made Laodicea a natural place for the establishment of a Christian church. Paul mentions Laodicea in his letter to the Colossians. "For I want you to know how great a struggle I have on your behalf and for those who are at Laodicea, and for all those who have not personally seen my face" (Colossians 2:1). "For I testify for him that he has a deep concern for you and for those who are in Laodicea and Hierapolis. Luke, the beloved physician, sends you his greetings, and also Demas. Greet the brethren who are in Laodicea and also Nympha and the church that is in her house. When this letter is read among you, have it also read in the church of the Laodiceans; and you, for your part read my letter that is coming from Laodicea" (Colossians 4:13–16).

Again, the message to the church at Laodicea comes from Jesus. He describes Himself as the one who has the final say, who sees everything but never lies and has been here since time began. We cannot fool Jesus. He knows our hearts and minds. "And Jesus knowing their thoughts said, 'Why are you thinking evil in your hearts?'" (Matthew 9:4). He sees not just our visible actions but also the unseen motives of the heart. The Laodiceans were going through the motions, but their hearts were not involved. They are neither "hot nor cold," without passion or love of God in their worship or lives. Because of their lack of love and devotion, they are lukewarm and unacceptable to Christ.

The earthly wealth they had gained from trade did not give them treasure in heaven and their eye salve did not help them see what they were lacking in their souls. Their famous textiles did not hide their shame from God. Jesus called them wretched, miserable, poor, blind, and naked. They were in a sorry state and did not even know it. This message was their warning and their call to change.

Jesus offers them the wealth of His love and the covering of His blood. His message is sent to give them the knowledge that they need His love and sacrifice to cover their sins. They are advised to listen, or they will face the discipline of their maker. A renewed zeal in what they are doing will bring them back into the grace of Jesus. Jesus is knocking at the door. He is in their presence ready to act if they will not repent. The next move is theirs.

Jesus is knocking on each of our doors. We all have a need to do more and to do it better. When we let Jesus into our lives and hearts, life becomes a celebration feast. We have riches greater than gold, clothing finer than any cloth, and vision that lets us see the glory and beauty of God. When we dine with Jesus, we truly have a feast made in heaven.

Overcoming the world requires being able to see beyond the treasures found on the earth. We must look beyond earthly fame and wealth and see the true riches of God. Paul said he counted all things rubbish so he can obtain Christ. "More than that, I count all things to be loss in view of the surpassing value of knowing Christ Jesus my Lord, for whom I have suffered the loss of all things, and count them but rubbish so that I may gain Christ" (Philippians 3:8). To overcome the world, we must value knowing Christ above everything else.

Each church has received a different message yet there is something in each message for all of us. We might need the message about passion one day and the next day our need might be for the encouragement Jesus sent to Philadelphia. Just as each message ends with the phrase "Let him that has an ear hear," we have a need to listen to all the words of our Creator and Savior. As Peter said, where else can we go for life? "Simon Peter answered Him, 'Lord, to whom shall we go? You have words of eternal life'" (John 6:68). In Christ, and in Him alone, dwells salvation.

CHAPTER 4

A VISIT TO THE
THRONE OF GOD

If the visions of the book are predictions of specific events in future human history, what is the message for us? How does a vision of a known accepted event fit in the middle of future events? How does knowing the specific events in the future help those who live before the event or after the event? On the other hand, knowing the involvement of Christ in creation from the beginning of creation until the end of time will strengthen our faith in His promise to return and bring us to dwell with Him.

As we look into the throne room of God, what do we see? Who is there? What are the beings there doing? Why is there a sea in front of the throne? Why are there thunder and lightning? What does this vision tell us about God the Father?

A Vision Outside of Time

Revelation, the book of visions, begins after the death and resurrection of Jesus. The messages to the seven churches are given during the last part of apostle John's life. This may lead us to look to the future for the rest of the visions. However, there is a vision of the birth of Jesus found in the middle of John's visions.

As we move forward through this book, we encounter a vision of the birth of Jesus in chapter 12. The birth of Jesus took place before the letters written to the seven churches. At some point, the visions go back in time to before the birth in Bethlehem. A common effect for movies and television shows is starting in the middle of the story and then jumping back to the beginning with a caption on the screen giving a time frame (six months earlier, etc.). How far back do the visions of this book go? To the beginning of the story? To the beginning of creation itself?

Before we were created, God and Jesus existed. The plan of salvation was an idea in the mind of God before He spoke the world into existence. The authority and worship of God began before the creation of men. When there were no people, there was God. When there was no sin, there was God. Chapter 4 takes John (and us) back to before the beginning of creation. "In the beginning God created the heavens and the earth" (Genesis 1:1). Here we will see God before creation. God in all His glory. God displayed in a grandeur that is described in such a way that men can understand. This vision is before the vision of Christ's birth (chapter 12) and before the plan of God is opened (chapter 5). Our world does not exist. Death and poverty do not yet exist (chapter 6).

The Throne Room of God: Revelation 4:1–11

This vision begins with an open door and an invitation to God's throne room (v. 1). Since flesh and blood cannot be in heaven, John is in the spirit going through the door to God's throne. "Now I say this, brethren, that flesh and blood cannot inherit the kingdom of God; nor does the perishable inherit the imperishable" (1 Corinthians 15:50). When John passes through the door, he sees a throne occupied by a magnificent being (v. 2). This is God the Father. Who else would be sitting on a throne in heaven? John's description is an attempt to describe that which cannot be described. He uses earthly beauty like jewels and rainbows to depict the glory he sees. There is nothing else he can use because people (including John) are only familiar with the world we live in. This truth also applies to the other beings John sees around the throne and in heaven. We can only describe what we see by using the things that are familiar. To describe color to the blind, we resort to the things we feel by touch. To describe sound to the deaf, we use sight and the feel of vibrations. To talk of adult things to a child, we use simple speech and examples of things in their world.

The Throne: Revelation 4:1–3

The throne depicts authority. The one seated on the throne has authority over all who come before him. More than a king, His word is law. The throne is filled with such power that thunder and lightning come from the throne. The light in the room is from lamps described as the seven spirits of God. Everything begins and ends here. This is the center of all that surrounds it. There is a sea of glass surrounding the throne making it hard to approach. Only the worthy can draw near. Those between the throne and the sea are not cowering in fear but are rejoicing and worshiping their King.

The Twenty-Four Elders: Revelation 4:4

God, on His throne, is surrounded by different inhabitants of heaven. Surrounding God's throne are twenty-four elders sitting on twenty-four thrones (v. 4). The most common religious authority figures in the Israel of John's time were the city elders. *Elders* is also the title given to the spiritual leaders of the local churches following Jesus. The gold crowns show these heavenly beings are an extension of God's authority, and the white robes show they are worthy. The number twelve shows up in a significant manner throughout the scriptures. There are twelve sons of Israel that father the twelve tribes of Israel. Later there are twelve apostles that are given authority by Jesus to bind and loose. Together they make twenty-four extensions of God's authority on earth and reflect the authority of these twenty-four elders.

The Thunder and Lightning: Revelation 4:5

The lightning and thunder coming from God's throne show the power and might of the Lord God. Nothing common in nature is more mysterious and powerful than thunder and lightning. Lighting and the following sound of thunder can strike fear into the hearts of men and animals. No one wants to be caught unprotected in a thunderstorm. It is a reminder of how helpless we can be in the face of nature. In this vision, it is a reminder of the awesome power of God. Those close to the thundering throne are not in fear but are engaged in praise of the one who sits in control of such awesome power.

The Seven Lamps: Revelation 4:5

Seven very bright lamps are blazing before the throne. The number seven always references God in some way. Seven has been the number for God ever since He rested after creation. The observance of the sabbath day by the Hebrews was a reminder that God made them and the world. Some translations render this as the "sevenfold Spirit of God." Seven lamps giving forth a light that shines on God the Father and on those who are worshiping Him.

The Sea of Glass: Revelation 4:6

In front of the throne is a large sea of glass. This sea surrounds the throne. It is a barrier to any not already within the space before God. A sea that separates any outside its boundary from God the Father.

At the time of this vision, men had been making glass for three thousand years. Around the time of Christ's birth, men learned the art of glass blowing. Glass was around but was far from common. It was for the wealthy; the poor were perhaps more familiar with crystal. Crystal or glass, the sea is a symbol of separation from God's throne. It is described as a sea and not a pool or even a pond or lake, making it difficult to cross.

This sea is copied in the Hebrew worship structure. "Therefore it was necessary for the copies of the things in the heavens to be cleansed with these, but the heavenly things themselves with better sacrifices than these. For Christ did not enter a holy place made with hands, a mere copy of the true one, but into heaven itself, now to appear in the presence of God for us" (Hebrews 9:23–24). A bronze sea is a part of the tabernacle that was created from God's instructions. The tabernacle was created as a place for the Israelites to worship and be close to God. "Moreover, he made the laver of bronze with its base of bronze, from the mirrors of the serving women who served at the doorway of the tent of meeting" (Exodus 38:8).

This sea was also a part of the temple built by Solomon. "Now he made the sea of cast metal ten cubits from brim to brim, circular in form, and its height was five cubits, and thirty cubits in circumference. Under its brim gourds went around encircling it ten to a cubit, completely surrounding the sea; the gourds were in two rows, cast with the rest. It stood on twelve oxen, three facing north, three facing west, three facing south, and three facing east; and the sea was set on top of them, and all their rear parts turned inward. It was a handbreadth thick, and its brim was made like the brim of a cup, as a lily blossom; it could hold two thousand baths" (1 Kings 7:23–26). This sea was between the people and the Holy of Holies, which contained the holy seat of God. Only the anointed and cleansed high priest was allowed to pass beyond this sea.

The Four Creatures: Revelation 4:6–11

The four creatures, full of eyes and in shapes described by John as creatures of the earth, were closer to the throne. Full of eyes, they would see everything. Seeing everything, they were praising God without stopping. Their words called God holy, mighty, and eternal. And when they spoke, the elders would bow down and worship Him. Then the elders would proclaim God the Creator and proclaim His worthiness to receive glory and honor and praise. This part of the vision shows the love and adoration given to God the Father from the beings that live with Him.

There is a lot of discussion about the four living creatures. Are they the same creatures in Ezekiel's vision? Are they different creatures but of the same family? Do they represent specific elements of spirit or creation? To understand their part in this vision, we do not need answers to these questions. The words describing this vision give them a place of honor and power near the throne of God. Their whole being, in this vision, is dedicated to worship and adoration of God on the throne. When a heavenly being is found worthy of opening the scroll in God's hand, the same worship and adoration is directed to that heavenly being described as a lamb that was slain.

CHAPTER 5

A PLAN FOR CREATION

What do we see in God's hand? Why is it significant? Why is the scroll sealed? Why is it so hard to open? Why does it take a special being to open the scroll? If Jesus is seated on the right hand of God, why do they search through heaven to find Him? Why is there great joy when someone is found to open the scroll? What is this new song of praise heard in heaven?

The Scroll: Revelation 5:1–8

In God's hand is a paper, scroll, or book that contains information hidden by seven seals. At this point, the contents of the scroll could be anything. It will only become known after all the seals are broken. What has this mighty and worthy God conceived? No one will know until the seals are broken. The seals are keeping the ideas written in this scroll hidden. They must be broken for the words of the scroll to be revealed. The things written there will remain a mystery until the seals are broken. Remember the power in the words of God the Creator? He spoke and His words became reality. "Then God said, 'Let there be light'; and there was light" (Genesis 1:3).

Who will break the seals? As the scene unfolds, no one is found worthy to break the seals. This realm of God is filled with powerful angels and magnificent spiritual beings. God's plan is waiting and ready. It only needs someone to take the scroll and open it to reveal the wonders it contains. No one is found. This scroll is written for a single special spirit. Only that spirit can open this scroll. John weeps as a search is launched. In all of heaven, is there anyone who can open the scroll and make the ideas from the mind of God come into being? One heavenly being is found worthy and is seen by John as a lamb that has been slain.

Those familiar with the scriptures and the story of Jesus will all reach the same conclusion. This is Jesus shown in a manner that will create instant recognition. This is Jesus Christ, the Lion of Judah, the promised Messiah. But it is Jesus before the scroll is opened. It is Jesus before the birth that takes place in chapter 12. When we watch old movies and catch familiar faces, we often name them by a role they will play later in their life. A story of George Washington as a boy might be titled "The Childhood of President Washington." Real people and fictional characters are often identified by symbols or traits. A favorite football player's nickname and a political figure depicted in a cartoon are two examples. Jesus is shown in this vision as the slain lamb so that He is readily identified as the breaker of the seals. The seals are not yet broken and Jesus has yet to be born in the flesh. The scroll is in His hand. He is worthy and able to bring the mystery that it contains into the light and the plans written there into existence.

The New Song: Revelation 5:9–14

The living creatures sing a new song. "And they sang a new song, saying, 'Worthy are You to take the book and to break its seals; for You were slain, and purchased for God with Your blood men from every tribe and tongue and people and nation. You have made them to be a kingdom and priests to our God; and they will reign upon the earth'" (Revelation 5:9–10). The words of this song speak of the great deeds Jesus is known for and clarify for John and his readers that this is indeed the Jesus he knows and loves. Heaven, however, is not bound by time as we are. The song describes the great deeds Jesus has accomplished and will accomplish that make Him worthy of praise and honor. He is worthy to open the scroll in God's hand. Because He is worthy and able, it is the same as if the scroll is already open.

Jesus has already stated to John that He is the Alpha and the Omega. Paul says all things have been created by Him, through Him, and for Him. "For by Him all things were created, *both* in the heavens and on earth, visible and invisible, whether thrones or dominions or rulers or authorities—all things have been created through Him and for Him" (Colossians 1:16). The creation story in Genesis says, "Let Us make man in Our image," and that phrase is widely accepted as including Jesus. The lamb that was slain is Jesus, in the beginning before creation, identified using present-day descriptions. As we watch the seals broken and the contents of the scroll revealed, we will see God's great plan for man unfold. Beginning from creation until man's final arrival in the eternal dwelling place of God, this mighty work of God is accomplished by His only begotten Son, Jesus.

CHAPTER 6

CHRIST BREAKS THE SEALS, CREATION BEGINS

Why is each seal broken separately? What does each seal reveal from the scroll? How long have the things revealed by the breaking of the scroll been a part of our world? Where are the things released from the scroll appearing? How long does the breaking of each seal take?

As each of the seals is broken, there appears a part of creation that makes up our world. Except for the short stay in the garden, where death was only a possibility, death has been a part of creation. The conflict represented by the red horseman has also been a constant part of creation. Adversity and desire as well as conflict and struggle all result from the free will of men. Free will includes the ability to disobey God. The consequence of that disobedience is death. Also, from the beginning has been God's plan of salvation. The tree of life was in the garden along with the possibility of dying.

The First Seal: Revelation 6:1–2

When the first seal is broken, a rider on a white horse appears. White is the color of purity, and the rider is given a golden crown. He is shown in majesty and glory. Filled with authority, He rides forth conquering. This is the picture of an unconquerable king. This is the role of God's spirit in His new creation before there is sin in the world.

The Second Seal: Revelation 6:3–4

The breaking of the second seal releases a rider on a red horse. He is given the power to destroy peace on the earth. The red of this horse is the same color as the dragon in chapter 12 that waged war in heaven. That dragon is named Satan or the devil. The adversary has certainly been here since the beginning. He is seen first in scripture as a snake tempting Eve and was successful in destroying the peace between God and Man. "The serpent said to the woman, 'You surely will not die!'" (Genesis 3:4). "And he laid hold of the dragon, the serpent of old, who is the devil and Satan, and bound him for a thousand years" (Revelation 20:2). Satan has been at work throughout time creating strife between God and man and between man and man.

The Third Seal: Revelation 6:5–6

Seal number three is broken, and a third horseman rides out holding in his hand the means of measuring or limiting the needs of humankind. Some call this horseman "famine," but scales can measure a little or a lot. A voice in the background ties the needs of men to money. Not just the food but also oil and wine. This represents the economy of the world from the simple needs of Adam to the money markets of today. This represents the treasures of the world shown to Jesus during his temptation and the Babylon seen later in John's visions. Man has struggled for survival and the accumulation of riches ever since leaving the garden. Material things are at the core of the struggle between Cain and his brother Abel.

The Fourth Seal: Revelation 6:7–8

Included in the creation story is the fall of man. Sin and death entered the world during the life of Adam. Paul teaches in Romans that like

Adam, all men sin, and all men die. "Therefore, just as through one man sin entered into the world, and death through sin, and so death spread to all men, because all sinned" (Romans 5:12). This is represented by the ashen horseman, Death. Death appears with the breaking of the fourth seal. Since Adam, men have never known a world without death and never known a world without sin.

The Fifth Seal: Revelation 6:9–11

The breaking of the fifth seal introduces martyrs. The first recorded death is that of Abel. He was slain for his righteousness by his brother Cain. People have been killed for their faith throughout history. "They were stoned, they were sawn in two, they were tempted, they were put to death with the sword; they went about in sheepskins, in goatskins, being destitute, afflicted, ill-treated (men of whom the world was not worthy), wandering in deserts and mountains and caves and holes in the ground)" (Hebrews 11:37–38). Jesus was crucified for His teaching. The apostles who followed Jesus were also persecuted and killed for their faith.

The Sixth Seal: Revelation 6:12–17

As the sixth seal is broken terror enters the world. With creation comes the struggle with Satan. He was there in the beginning to sow discord between God and man. When this seal is broken, sin comes to creation, and with sin, judgment. The breaking of this seal, because of the free will of man and the consequences of wrong choices, reveals the wrath of God. Forgiveness and judgment are both necessary parts of creation. Earth is shaken. Both day and night are places of terror. There is no escaping the wrath of God. With sin (separation from God) comes the consequences. Remember Adam hid in the bushes instead of facing God. A person's rank or economic status does not protect them from God's wrath. The only salvation lies in Jesus. Just as judgment comes at the beginning of creation, so does a plan for forgiveness. Forgiveness will enter the world at a great cost.

CHAPTER 7

THERE IS A PAUSE
IN HEAVEN

Why is there a pause before opening the seventh seal? What is seen before the seventh seal is opened? Are the things released by opening the first seals good things? If there are only the results of opening the first six seals in human history, where is God's love?

Before the Last Seal

Between the sixth and seventh seals is a break. During this break, John sees angels holding back the destruction that is facing the earth because of man's sin. The breaking of the first six seals releases enough unrighteousness to bring about the destruction of the earth and all humankind. There is no apparent reason for the world to continue. But God has included in His scroll a plan that will rescue men from sin. The God of love has commanded the angels to hold back from destroying the earth until He has sealed those who will accept salvation. There is still one seal left before God's plan has completely unfolded. His salvation (sealing the foreheads of God's bond servants) will include both Jews and Gentiles. This vision gives a glimpse ahead to the end of the story.

A Beginning of God's Plan for Man: Revelation 7:1–3

There are two groups introduced here in chapter 7. Both groups are sealed to God and represent those who accept God's promises and leadership. Both groups will be sealed before the destruction of the earth. Everything that God has created has been created to produce the people represented by these two groups. All of the horsemen and the struggle they represent will bring testing and strength to produce those sealed to God.

The 144,000: Revelation 7:4–8

The first group is described by a number, 144,000. The twelve tribes of Israel are named, telling John and the reader that these are the people sealed under God's promise to Abraham. This number is not meant to be an accurate figure but to show a completed number. All the people of all the tribes (or twelve times twelve) becomes 144,000. At the time of John's visions, those saved under the Jewish law were already numbered. Jesus said He came not to abolish the law but to fulfill the law. "Do not think that I came to abolish the Law or the Prophets; I did not come to abolish but to fulfill" (Matthew 5:17). While we live in a world where time moves in only one direction, God is not limited by time. He already knew the end of the story because He wrote the scroll.

The Great Multitude: Revelation 7:9–17

The second group is a great multitude not yet numbered. They are from every nation on earth. They are described as having escaped from a great tribulation. Their tribulation is not one specific event, but the term is descriptive of all the dangers and struggles God's people face throughout all ages. They have escaped through the sacrifice of Jesus the Lamb and pay tribute for their salvation to God the Father and Jesus the Lamb. John is asked, "Who are they and where do they come from?" The question is asked and answered by one of the elders. This multitude of people is known in heaven, and their method of salvation is also known. He is then told that they are the ones who have been redeemed by washing their robes in the blood of the Lamb. (The Christ that is born in chapter 12.) He is given a very descriptive picture of their future by the angel directing his vision. This description makes very clear their joy and the role of Jesus in their salvation. They worship God with the same reverence as the four creatures and the twenty-four elders. And God's love and care is given to them as the love and care of a father to beloved children.

CHAPTER 8

BREAKING THE LAST SEAL

After the interlude in chapter 7, the last seal is broken. How is the breaking of this seal different from the last six? Why is there silence in heaven? What happens as the scroll is opened? When the scroll is open, why is the vision not finished? What happens now? Why trumpets? What are they calling attention too? As the trumpets sound, one-third of creation is affected. Why one-third? Why are there three woes? Are the three woes paired with the three periods of God's interaction with men?

The Last Seal: Revelation 8:1–2

The vision then continues with the Lamb breaking the seventh and last seal on the scroll or book. When the last seal is broken, silence falls in heaven. It is the silence of waiting and expectation. It is the hush before the roar. The scroll is open; great events are about to take place. The plan of God is revealed. The words on the scroll are known and have become reality. Creation is born.

Redemption Begins: Revelation 8:1–2

As the scroll unrolls, seven angels appear with seven trumpets. Trumpets are used to herald people or events or to give commands. Each angel will announce a different part of God's salvation plan. Remember destruction is being held back until the sealing of the saints—both Abraham's descendants and the great multitude. Adam has sinned and death has entered the new creation, but God's plan for the salvation of souls is beginning. "And I will put enmity between you and the woman, and between your seed and her seed; He shall bruise you on the head, and you shall bruise him on the heel" (Genesis 3:15). This is said to be the first promise of the Christ that was to come and save the souls of men.

The Golden Censer: Revelation 8:3–5

Complete destruction is held back, but the conflict between evil and righteousness still fills the earth. Men will desire good and will reach toward God in prayer. Good men will face evil men. Good men will strive with evil in the spirit world and within themselves. It is to rescue these good souls that God holds back destruction.

Before the first trumpet sounds, an angel appears with a golden censer filled with incense and the prayers of the saints. The censer was included in the tabernacle and temple worship of the Israelites. It was used to produce a cleansing and a pleasant odor for worship. The prayers of God's saints are pleasant to Him. After the smoke rises before God, the censer is cast to earth with thunder and lightning and causes an earthquake.

The prayers of the saints contribute to God's wrath against the world. Those who praise God are a sharp contrast to those who do not praise God. Those who serve God by serving others are a sharp contrast to those who hurt others to serve themselves. Judgment will include an example of what men could be so that what they are becomes evident by comparison. Jesus is an example of goodness that shines its light on evil. Good men show evil for what it is.

The Sounding of the Trumpets: Revelation 8:6

The first trumpet sounds and one-third of the earth (ground) is destroyed by fire and hail. When the second angel sounds, one-third of the sea becomes void of life. When the third trumpet sounds, a great star falls from heaven to the earth and a third of the fresh water is made bitter. (The first chapter states that the stars represent angels.) The fourth trumpet sounds and a third of the heavens are darkened. Just the creation of a plan to save men will doom a third of creation. Man's sin has far-reaching consequences. With creation comes the adversary. That dragon of old, Satan, was there on the first day of creation seeking how he might take the glory of God for himself. Remember the second horseman that appears at the very beginning of seal breaking (6:4). The fifth trumpet sees the star that has fallen from heaven bound and limited in his actions. The star has power, but that power is limited by the God who holds all power. Just as we see destruction happening to one-third of creation, we also see God preserving two-thirds of creation from that destruction. God will hold back the destruction of creation until He has sealed all the souls who will accept His forgiveness.

The First Trumpet: Revelation 8:7

The vision of the first trumpet sounding is descriptive of the fall of man. Satan is involved (the star wormwood). The earth is affected, and the ground is cursed. Then to Adam He said, "Because you have listened to the voice of your wife, and have eaten from the tree about which I commanded you, saying, 'You shall not eat from it'; Cursed is the ground because of you; In toil you will eat of it all the days of your life. "Both thorns and thistles it shall grow for you; And you will eat the plants of the field (Genesis 3:17–18). "How long is the land to mourn. And the vegetation of the countryside to wither? For the wickedness of those who dwell in it, animals and birds have been snatched away, because men have said, 'He will not see our latter ending'" (Jeremiah 12:4). Humankind no longer has the advantage of direct communication with God and must struggle for survival.

Humans' troubles began in the garden when Adam separated himself from God because of disobedience. "He said, 'I heard the sound of You in the garden, and I was afraid because I was naked; so I hid myself'" (Genesis 3:10). That separation from God brought about the struggles men have with the earth, sea, and sky. Life without God is hard, and humankind must learn that God is necessary to life before he can be salvaged or redeemed. "That they would seek God, if perhaps they might grope for Him and find Him, though He is not far from each one of us; for in Him we live and move and exist, as even some of your own poets have said, 'For we also are His children'" (Acts 17:27–28).

The Second Trumpet: Revelation 8:8

A great burning mountain is cast into the sea. The sea becomes corrupt and one-third of the sea turns into blood. Not just the land but also the sea is affected by the fall of man. When the ground is cursed with thorns and thistles, man has not yet turned to the sea for survival. When men finally reach the sea for a livelihood, they will find the sea also has its difficulties and dangers.

The Third Trumpet: Revelation 8:10–11

The sound of the third trumpet brings bitterness to the fresh water men need to survive. Wormwood was used to treat intestinal worms and was very bitter and hard to swallow. Life after the fall will not be easy anywhere on the earth. The sinful nature of man given free reign will bring strife and conflict into nature and even with nature itself. There is nowhere people can turn for peace and comfort except to God.

The Fourth Trumpet: Revelation 8:12

The fourth trumpet brings darkness. One-third of light and its sources are lost. When Adam hid from God, he did not want God to see him. Because of sin, much of God's glory must be hidden from men. Sin cannot bear the light of truth. When Jesus came to our world, He brought a new vision of God's glory. A vision that sinful man could behold and cling to. A vision of hope and a way to return to God's presence. "I have come as Light into the world, so that everyone who believes in Me will not remain in darkness" (John 12:46). There is no part of the world of men that sin has not tainted.

Between Trumpets Four and Five

The first four trumpets show the effects sin has on God's creation. If there was no sin (separation of man from God), the world could be like the Garden of Eden. The world would be a pleasant place to live. God's presence would be a part of everyone's life. Before there is salvation, there is danger. Without danger, there would be no need for salvation. Man's greatest danger is his denial of God and the goodness God represents. Without righteousness, there is no reason for creation to continue. "Then the Lord saw that the wickedness of man was great on the earth, and that every intent of the thoughts of his heart was only evil continually. The Lord was sorry that He had made man on the earth, and He was grieved in His heart. The Lord said, 'I will blot out man whom I have created from the face of the land, from man to animals to creeping things and to birds of the sky; for I am sorry that I have made them.' But Noah found favor in the eyes of the Lord" (Genesis 6:5–8).

The Three Woes: Revelation 8:13

Between the fourth and fifth trumpets sounding, an eagle flies through the midheaven, declaring three woes. The term *midheaven* is found three times in John's visions (Revelation 8:13, 14:6, and 19:17). In all three visions, the messenger is flying or calling on birds that fly. This is an area or space that is separate from earth but close to earth like the sky. It is in the spiritual realm but adjacent to our physical world. Here we first hear of the three woes that come upon man.

There are three woes because there are three major divisions in the salvation of men. Man on his own is doomed. (The flood.) Man failing to follow God's law is doomed. (The fall of Israel.) Man rejecting God's grace is doomed. (The end of time.) Woe is a necessary part of salvation. While some men are plucked from the destruction sin brings to the world, there will always be others who refuse to accept God's mercy. The woes began with the sounding of the last three trumpets announcing God's salvation. Some will escape from woe because they hear the trumpet and recognize the danger; others will embrace the ways of the world and not desire rescue. In the days of Noah, there was only one ark. Woe to those who were not aboard.

In the days of the Israelites, there were those who wanted a god that they could see and touch. Woe to those who worshiped that which was not the true God. In the days of Christ, not all listened and repented, but those men who preferred the world over God crucified Him. Woe to men who reject Jesus and choose the world instead of God. In our present time, people still reject God. Seeking to replace God with human ideals or religions that cater to human desires. Men also deny the existence of God and replace God with scientific theories and facts found in nature. Magic, luck, and fate replace faith and prayer.

CHAPTER 9

THE ADVERSARY
MOVES TO CREATION

Who is this star that falls from heaven? What is the bottomless pit? Who does God seal from the destruction? What are these strange creatures that attack men? What is the first woe that is past? Who is the army from the east? Why is there only one-third killed and the rest spared?

The Fifth Trumpet: Revelation 9:1–12

When the fifth trumpet sounds, the devil, who has fallen to earth, releases all the evil that men face, both the visible and the unseen. The descriptive imagery of the vision depicts the horror of evil. The locusts coming out of the pit are described as horses that combine the features of men, women, and beasts. Satan uses them all to cause misery to humankind. Only those sealed by God are immune from this destruction. Five months is the set time for this destruction to happen. The importance of the time is not the number or the quantity but the fact that it is set and limits the length of this destruction.

Evil is restrained by God and not allowed free reign. Creation will not be destroyed by the evil the fallen angel has released. Satan is limited and restrained by God from the moment he is cursed in the garden. Satan can only work under that restraint. His power is limited by God. "'Have You not made a hedge about him and his house and all that he has, on every side? You have blessed the work of his hands, and his possessions have increased in the land. But put forth Your hand now and touch all that he has; he will surely curse You to Your face.' Then the LORD said to Satan, 'Behold, all that he has is in your power, only do not put forth your hand on him.' So Satan departed from the presence of the LORD" (Job 1:10–12). People God claims as His own are protected. Satan has never had and never will have enough power to resist God.

All this evil comes out of the bottomless pit, the abyss. All this evil has been released into creation by the fallen angel. The key that opens the abyss is the temptation placed before Adam in the garden. Adam became aware of his own nakedness but did not see the full extent of the evil that had come into the world. The battle between good and evil is fought both in the temporal world and in a world we do not see. "For our struggle is not against flesh and blood, but against the rulers, against the powers, against the world forces of this darkness, against the spiritual forces of wickedness in the heavenly places" (Ephesians 6:12).

All the effects of evil are not visible to the human eye. When a man tells a lie resulting in someone's death, the death is only part of the story. One man may die, which we see, but another man has caused destruction to his soul, which we do not see. The grief for the man killed is also brought into the lives of people who cared. Grief can also come to the family and friends of the killer. Adam (humankind), with a recent knowledge of good and evil, is like a child that only knows he has displeased his parents and does not see the far-reaching effects of his actions.

Satan has been working to separate God from humankind in this world ever since he spoke to Eve in the garden. He works in the shadows whispering lies and stirring division among people. Satan delights in wars and in murders. Turmoil and chaos give the devil pleasure, and he works endlessly to create hate and fear. Every evil in the world, from the old Roman crucifixions to modern-day mass shootings, can be laid at his feet. We do not see Satan but deal with his influence every day. Our only protection comes from God. One of Satan's most successful methods of separating us from God's love is doubt. Is there really a God? Does God care about someone like me? If He is a God of love, why does He allow all this evil to happen? John's visions hold the answers to these questions.

The First Woe: Revelation 9:12

The numbers in this vision are only symbolic and are not an actual count. The army is a vision of terror, not a real army but an army out of a nightmare. An army born of man's terror. One-third of humankind is lost because this is the first of three woes. Each woe takes its toll on humankind and those lost are spoken of as one-third. This first woe ends when the earth is flooded and only Noah and his family are rescued. "Behold, I, even I am bringing the flood of water upon the earth, to destroy all flesh in which is the breath of life, from under heaven; everything that is on the earth shall perish. But I will establish My covenant with you; and you shall enter the ark—you and your sons and your wife, and your sons' wives with you" (Genesis 6:17–18).

There are others sealed during this interval. Enoch was from this phase of salvation. "So all the days of Enoch were three hundred and sixty-five years. Enoch walked with God; and he was not, for God took him" (Genesis 5:23–24).

Destruction is not complete because the earth itself is spared and the animals are saved in the ark. After the flood, the plants again return. The saved animals multiply and replenish the earth. Men and their wives have children.

When humankind again spreads over the face of God's creation, the lesson of the flood is forgotten. Once again man endeavors to replace God by worshiping what is not God. Idols become an excuse to behave according to man's own desires. The third horseman still works in men's hearts. Man, on his own, cannot find his way back to God. "I know, O LORD, that a man's way is not in himself, Nor is it in a man who walks to direct his steps" (Jeremiah 10:23). At this point in history, God will begin to teach men His law and love. The first woe has come because men reject God and righteousness when left to their own resources.

The Sixth Trumpet: Revelation 9:13–11:21

The sixth trumpet sounds after the first woe is past. The earth has been repopulated and the plan for salvation will move forward. Man cannot rule himself because his desires lead him to self-destruct. When men are left to their own resources without a guide, they will never find their way. "I know, O Lord, that a man's way is not in himself, nor is it in a man who walks to direct his steps" (Jeremiah 10:23).

The sixth trumpet announces the beginning of a planned event. The four angels were prepared for this before it happened. This is not God working "plan B" but is a part of the original scroll. Four angels are released, indicating the four directions of the compass—meaning all the earth is involved. There is a dividing of humankind. A portion of humankind is condemned, and the rest of humankind is called to repent. They are accused of idol worship, murder, sorcery, and theft. Horses, similar to the locusts from the previous vision, are now the instruments of man's grief. From their mouths comes forth smoke described as three plagues: fire, smoke, and brimstone. Fire that burns, smoke that chokes, and brimstone that consumes.

The Making of Israel: Revelation 10:1–11:14

Men in the days following the great flood soon fell back into trying to live by their own wisdom and forsaking God. The drunkenness of Noah, the confusing of language, the calling of Abraham, and the destruction of Sodom and Gomorrah all happen during this period following the great flood. Stories of the great flood are a part of man's history. Records of the flood are found in many places recorded in many languages. Legends and tales from many historic cultures describe a great flood. Yet people fell away from God. They worshiped idols they created with their own minds and hands. Or they worshiped themselves, living for the pleasures found in this world. Pleasures that Satan made attractive to men in his desire to replace worship of God with worship of himself.

The patriarchs—Abraham, Isaac, and Jacob—were called and led by God to establish a nation that would be separate from the world and worship and serve Him. "By faith Abraham, when he was called, obeyed by going out to a place which he was to receive for an inheritance; and he went out, not knowing where he was going. By faith he lived as an alien in the land of promise, as in a foreign land, dwelling in tents with Isaac and Jacob, fellow heirs of the same promise; for he was looking for the city which has foundations, whose architect and builder is God" (Hebrews 11:8–10).

The descendants of Abraham would suffer years of slavery in Egypt and emerge as a large population of believers in the one true God. As slaves they have retained their identity as children of Abraham. They have grown into the size of a nation. They are people without rulers are laws. They are ready to be molded by God into a nation that will produce the Messiah that will bring salvation into the world.

CHAPTER 10

GOD INTRODUCES HIS LAW

What is this little book? Why is it described as little? Why is John told to eat the book? Why does it taste sweet but become bitter in the end? What is in the little book? How does the little book impact what God has created?

The Little Book: Revelation 10:1–8

Between the sixth and the last trumpet, an angel appears with a little book that is open. The angel is strong and majestic. He has the rainbow, God's promise, on his head. He is clothed in purity and has a face that is radiant like the sun as he becomes a messenger from God. The book is small because it contains only a portion of God's plan. The book being opened means it is in effect when this trumpet sounds. The size being mentioned implies there is a greater message that will come later.

The angel plants his feet and seven thunders speak from the throne of God. The thunder from God's throne shows the power behind the message delivered. John is told not to write them. The words that thunder from the throne will not be given to the world because the world is not ready. There are still parts of God's plan to unfold. The thunders may speak of the Christ to come. Paul teaches of a mystery revealed, which is the Gospel of

Christ. "Of this church I was made a minister according to the stewardship from God bestowed on me for your benefit, so that I might fully carry out the preaching of the word of God, that is, the mystery that has been hidden from the past ages and generations, but has now been manifested to His saints" (Colossians 1:25–26). The thunders could have spoken of Christ, who died at the "right time."

The Bitter Taste: Revelation 10:9–11

John is given the little book and commanded to swallow it. He finds the book sweet to the taste and very satisfying. When the book settles into John's stomach, however, it becomes bitter and unsettling. It proves to be unsatisfying and not sufficient for his hunger.

The book represents God's covenant with Abraham's children and the laws given to Moses to govern those children. The promise and the law seem to be all that man needs. But just as men could not govern themselves, they are also unable to live by the laws given them. The law is corrupted by man's fleshly nature and warped to fit his own desires.

The laws that God gives to Moses are soon broken and replaced with the "traditions of men." Even while Moses was on the mountain receiving God's commandments from God's own hand, the people fell away. In the shadow of God's cloud and the holy mountain, Aaron built for them a golden calf to replace the God that led them from Egypt. Even after the law was firmly in place, they grumbled and complained. The law and God's presence in the tabernacle were not enough. They grumbled and complained and were compelled to wander in the wilderness for forty years until a new generation that had not known Egypt was of age to follow God.

Even Moses, who had been with God on the mountain, fell short of God's glory. Having a law from God they failed to keep, they began to teach for law their own traditions. "Then the Lord said, 'Because this people draw near with their words and honor Me with their lip service, But they remove their hearts far from Me, and their reverence for Me consists of tradition learned by rote, Therefore behold, I will once again deal marvelously with this people, wondrously marvelous; And the wisdom of their wise men will perish, and the discernment of their discerning men will be concealed'" (Isaiah 29:13–14).

CHAPTER 11

THE LAW SERVES
ITS PURPOSE

Why does John measure the temple? Why is John told not to measure the outer court? Who are the two witnesses? Which Bible character changed water into blood? Which prophet prayed for there to be no rain? How can fire come from a prophet's mouth? Who is the beast that comes out of the abyss? How does he make war on the prophets? When the seventh trumpet sounds, why are there joy and worship around God's throne?

Measuring the Temple: Revelation 11:1–2

John is commanded to measure the temple and the people who worship there because this part of God's plan is complete. You cannot measure what is not completed. The nation of Israel is established. The law of Moses is established and is limited in its duration because it is a tutor to bring the world to the next stage of God's plan, the Messiah. "Therefore the Law has become our tutor to lead us to Christ, so that we may be justified by faith. But now that faith has come, we are no longer under a tutor" (Galatians 3:24–25). When the next trumpet sounds, a new part of salvation's plan will begin. The Messiah, Jesus Christ, will arrive and begin the final part of God's plan for humankind.

The outer court is not measured because it is outside the law given to Moses by God and will be in opposition to Israel. This oppression will shape God's nation into a place suitable for the birth of Christ. The part that is measured is oppressed by the outer court that is not measured. This oppression will continue for a specific time. It is not necessary to define the forty-two months to understand the vision. (The number forty-two is six times seven. The number six represents man who falls short of God, and the number seven represents God in His completeness. The forty-two months is the time set by God and needed by man before the next part of God's great plan can begin.)

The specified time and the measuring of the temple indicate that the little book is limited in scope and duration. Throughout their history, the Hebrew people were often oppressed by their neighbors. They were led into captivity by God's hand, God using their oppressors to forge a nation where the world's Savior would come and begin His ministry. Shaped by oppression and triumph, the remnant of God's people became convinced there was only one God and that He would send a Messiah to redeem them. The birthplace of Jesus was being forged.

The Two Witnesses: Revelation 11:3–14

The two witnesses who are mentioned are not named but their description indicates Moses, who turned water into blood, and Elijah, whose prayer stopped the rain. Moses was the law giver, and Elijah was the most notable of the prophets. Together they represent the whole of God's instruction to the Hebrew people. Not only did they give God's law and instructions to the people but also the promise of God's blessing.

Their testimony continues after their passing from this earth and it is a constant source of irritation to the devil. The two witnesses are described as olive trees and lampstands, two common symbols from the scriptures. Olive trees were a big part of Hebrew culture. Olives were used as food, and the oil was used in ceremonies. The Hebrew people found use for the wood and even used the groves as shelter. The lampstand gives light and represents God's word. Jesus used the law and the prophets to explain His appearance on the earth. "Then beginning with Moses and with all the prophets, He explained to them the things concerning Himself in all the Scriptures" (Luke 24:27).

The Hebrews were God's people when they followed His teaching. These are the two named as being on the mount of transfiguration with Jesus. They were vital to the teaching of the Jews and heroes of the nation. Peter wants to build a tabernacle to each of these men and to Christ. At that moment, God speaks from heaven, declaring Jesus as His Son and spokesman. "Then a cloud formed, overshadowing them, and a voice came out of the cloud, 'This is My beloved Son, listen to Him!'" (Mark 9:7). Because they were seen with Christ, we know they were protected from their enemies and were conquerors of death through faith.

Sodom and Egypt are two of Satan's strongholds that troubled God's people. These two are named but represent all the places in the world where Satan's power rules. Sodom was a corrupt city in the days of Abraham. Lot, Abraham's nephew, was lured by the comforts of the city and later rescued. Many of Israel's troubles came from the descendants of Lot and his daughters. Egypt was a refuge for Abraham's grandson Jacob and his children but later held their descendants as slaves for more than four hundred years. Egypt is often used as a symbol of the oppression of God's people.

After their work is complete, the two witnesses are slain. Their teaching and prophecy are rejected by God's people and are replaced with the traditions of men. "He was also saying to them, 'You are experts at setting aside the commandment of God in order to keep your tradition'" (Mark 7:9). The three and a half days mark the completion of this part of God's plan. Their work done, they are gathered to God.

This also marks the completion of the second woe. The second woe marks the end of Israel as God's only people and culminates with the destruction of Jerusalem in AD 70. Those who failed to turn back to God under this covenant are doomed by their choices. The second woe has come upon man. God gave men laws and they could not live by law; instead, they rejected God, His law, and His righteousness.

The Last Trumpet: Revelation 11:15

The last trumpet sounds, announcing the final phase of God's plan for saving humankind. The voices of heaven declare that God's reign has come to the earth. The teaching prayer of Jesus included "thy kingdom come" and "thou will be done on earth as in heaven." This will be accomplished with the final phase of God's plan. The age of law and prophets ends and the reign of the Christ begins. The ending of the age of Moses and the prophets is seen by the appearance of the ark of God's covenant in heaven.

The kingdom of Christ will be revealed to the earth in all its glory. Beginning with His birth, Jesus ushers in a new era of God's relationship with humankind. His kingdom will not be a kingdom of law but a kingdom of kindred spirits. Spirits that put on the aspect of God and Christ are ruled not by laws but by love. "By this all men will know that you are My disciples, if you have love for one another" (John 13:35). As Christ speaks the words of His ministry, judgment is pronounced on all who reject the love of God and His Son.

The coming of Christ will limit the power of Satan even more than in the past. In the Gospels, we see Jesus cast out Satan's demons and correct many of the physical ills of this world caused by Satan's evil. Just as the world was spoken into existence, the reward for God's saints will become a reality with every word Jesus speaks.

The Last Trumpet Sounds: Revelation 11:15–19

The voices in heaven declare that God's has extended His kingdom into the world of men. This is the beginning of what Jesus prayed for in Matthew 6. "Thy kingdom come." The coming of Jesus brings judgment to those who follow Satan and reward to those who will follow Jesus. There is joy in heaven that God's predetermined plan of salvation has been set in place. God has opened a way for sinful men to approach His throne. This last trumpet announces the birth of our Savior!

CHAPTER 12

THE CONCEPTION
AND BIRTH OF JESUS

Who is the woman expecting a child? Who is the child? Who is the dragon? Why start a war in heaven? Who are the stars, and why do some of them side with the dragon? When they are cast out of heaven where do they go? Why does the dragon try to destroy the child and the woman?

A Woman Gives Birth: Revelation 12:1–2

The sounding of the last trumpet brings a new vision. This new vision starts with a woman clothed in celestial glory and expecting a child. She is beginning to experience labor pains. The woman represents the nation of Israel and the child to be born is the promised Messiah. God's people, Israel, have finally accepted that He is the only God, and they cry out to Him daily for the promised Savior. They expect a king to deliver them from Roman oppression, but God has a greater deliverance in mind.

The Dragon Attacks: Revelation 12:3–4

Beside the woman in labor appears a great red dragon with seven heads wearing a crown. The dragon has authority and a purpose that engulfs a third of the angels in heaven. "And the great dragon was thrown down, the serpent of old who is called the devil and Satan, who deceives the whole world; he was thrown down to the earth, and his angels were thrown down with him" (Revelation 12:9). The dragon is focused on destroying the woman's child. From the Roman oppression to the killing of the babies in Bethlehem, Satan does all that he can to destroy this child. "Then when Herod saw that he had been tricked by the magi, he became very enraged, and sent and slew all the male children who were in Bethlehem and all its vicinity, from two years old and under, according to the time which he had determined from the magi" (Matthew 2:16).

This is the apex of Satan's power. He brings all the power he can to bear on this moment in time. The angels cast out of heaven become demons unleashed among the people. People Satan can sway to do his will have been placed in positions of power. He is the prince of this world and uses all the influence that he can bring to stop God's plan from moving past this moment. He fails. "Now judgment is upon this world; now the ruler of this world will be cast out" (John 12:31). With the coming of Christ, his true nature is revealed, and with the resurrection of Christ, his power is limited more than ever before. The casting out of demons shows his weakness and restraint by God. "But no one can enter the strong man's house and plunder his property unless he first binds the strong man, and then he will plunder his house" (Mark 3:27). Hard as he may try, Satan will not win. Evil will be overcome. God will redeem His people.

A Child Is Born: Revelation 12:5–6

The child is born and immediately comes under God's protection. Described as ruling all nations with a rod of iron, this is the Christ, the Messiah, promised in prophecy: the King of Kings and Lord of Lords. "You shall break them with a rod of iron, You shall shatter them like earthenware" (Psalm 2:9). The dragon tries to destroy the child before

He can grow and fulfill God's prophecies. Remember prophecy is God stating what He will do. The dragon's attempt to destroy the child is a direct rebellion against God. Satan will no longer be allowed in heaven.

A War in Heaven: Revelation 12:7–9

The birth of the child sets off a war in heaven resulting in angels being cast out of heaven. These cast-out rebellious angels appear on earth as demons. Being from heaven, they knew Jesus, recognizing His authority. "Seeing Jesus, he cried out and fell before Him, and said in a loud voice, 'What business do we have with each other, Jesus, Son of the Most High God? I beg You, do not torment me'" (Luke 8:28). Satan's bid for power is lost here. He has been cast from heaven. He will not cease to battle, but it is a losing struggle.

Satan Attacks the Woman: Revelation 12:13–16

Unable to destroy the child, Satan makes a strong attempt to destroy the woman who gave birth (Israel). Soon after the resurrection of Jesus, the full wrath of Rome is brought to bear and Israel once again faces physical destruction. "Jesus came out from the temple and was going away when His disciples came up to point out the temple buildings to Him. And He said to them, 'Do you not see all these things? Truly I say to you, not one stone here will be left upon another, which will not be torn down'" (Matthew 24:1–2). This is the second of the three woes. The resurrection of Jesus marks the fulfilment of the law and prophets. God puts the woman (Israel) into safekeeping. Not the physical nation but the souls of those who have kept faith with his teaching.

This is the 144,000 who are sealed to God from the visions of chapters 7 and 14. "And I heard the number of those who were sealed, one hundred and forty-four thousand sealed from every tribe of the sons of Israel" (Revelation 7:4). This is not a literal number but a number that shows completeness. Not one of God's faithful will be overlooked.

Satan Changes His Tactics: Revelation 12:17

Satan then turns his evil intentions on the people who follow Jesus. Satan, the great accuser, works to discredit God's people just as he did with Job. God's people are clearly identified. Their strength of conviction is greater than their fear of death. Their loyalty is to the Lamb, even if it means their death. They keep the commandments of God and hold to the testimony of Jesus. We know them as Christians. The Christian battle is not against flesh and blood but against Satan and his followers. "For our struggle is not against flesh and blood, but against the rulers, against the powers, against the world forces of this darkness, against the spiritual forces of wickedness in the heavenly places" (Ephesians 6:12).

The seals are all broken and the trumpets have all sounded. The great plan of God has unfolded. Satan now sets out to destroy the church Jesus has bought with His blood. The rest of this book is about the battle between Christ, His followers, and the dragon, Satan. The remaining visions also show the final outcomes of this struggle. The images John sees can be confusing. They must be understood in the context of the battle of good and evil. Remember this is a revelation of Jesus Christ and not a guidebook of human history.

As each of the seals is broken, Christ is revealed as a part of the events seen in the visions. Riding the ark with Noah and crossing the miles with Abraham, Christ is involved. He was there with Moses when the Israelites wandered in the wilderness. "For I do not want you to be unaware, brethren, that our fathers were all under the cloud and all passed through the sea; and all were baptized into Moses in the cloud and in the sea; and all ate the same spiritual food; and all drank the same spiritual drink, for they were drinking from a spiritual rock which followed them; and the rock was Christ" (1 Corinthians 10:1–4). The remaining visions will show the fierceness of the enemy and the support God gives His people.

CHAPTER 13

SATAN MAKES WAR ON CHRISTIANS

How does a spirit make war on people of flesh? What does the vision of the beasts represent? Why are there two beasts? How are they different? How are they the same? What is the mark of the beast? Is the mark a real man or a representation of human evil?

The First Beast: Revelation 13:1–10

The dragon, Satan, stands on the shore of a sea. An earthly sea is a vast body of water that holds many mysteries. This sea represents Satan's power in the unseen world of spirits. From out of this sea, he calls forth a terrifying beast, The beast has ten horns and seven heads. The number of heads speaks of the spiritual realm and the ten horns represent four plus six. Four for the four corners of the earth (north, south, east, and west) and six for the number that falls short of God and is often used to symbolize man. Both are from the physical world and the two together are ten, a number for completeness.

The diadems are symbols of the authority given to the beast. The authority of this beast is given to him by the dragon and cannot exceed the freedom Satan is allowed by God. His appearance was that of powerful creatures of the earth. He had the appearance of having died and having come back to life. The false image of life conquering death.

The people of earth worshiped the dragon because of the appearance of the beast. His heads were covered with lies about the nature of God. He spoke lies to God's people to charm them away from following Christ. Remember that Satan is the father of lies, and this beast is no better. "You are of your father the devil, and you want to do the desires of your father. He was a murderer from the beginning, and does not stand in the truth because there is no truth in him. Whenever he speaks a lie, he speaks from his own nature, for he is a liar and the father of lies" (John 8:44). This beast will lure those who love the world and its treasures more than they love God and His virtues.

This first beast appeals to the fleshly nature of men, the lust of the flesh, the lust of the eyes, and the pride of life. "For all that is in the world, the lust of the flesh and the lust of the eyes and the boastful pride of life, is not from the Father, but is from the world" (1 John 2:16). Remember this beast's appeal comes from the dragon who has the power of this world's pleasures and riches. This beast offers much the same temptations to God's people as Satan offered to Jesus when He was tempted.

The lure of riches is not in the holding of wealth but in the lie that wealth will solve the soul's troubles. This is the beast that promises your life will be better when you have more money, enjoy more pleasure, or have more fame. In the end, wealth is left behind at death, pleasure does not last, and fame goes to someone new. The promises of this beast are empty and offer no lasting value and only serve to separate those who believe his lies from God the Father, who could save them.

The Second Beast: Revelation 13:11–15

The first beast is from the sea, and the second is from the earth. There is no place on earth, land, or sea where men can escape the beast and the influence of the dragon. Escape only lies in placing our trust in God and placing our citizenship in heaven. We battle things we cannot see with our eyes. We need the protection of God's armor as described in Ephesians 6.

"Therefore, take up the full armor of God, so that you will be able to resist in the evil day, and having done everything, to stand firm" (Ephesians 6:13). Faith and truth protect God's people from the devil's lies. The word of God is the only weapon that drives both beasts away and keeps them at bay.

The beast from the earth has a more deceiving appearance than the first beast. He rises from the earth looking like a lamb that was slain. Indeed, he mimics the appearance of the true lamb of God, Jesus. The purpose of this beast is to direct worship from God to the first beast. This worship has the appearance of godliness but is just another form of love of the world. The deception is so complete that men will attribute signs and miracles to this beast and become even more convinced to accept the lies and deception he uses.

This religious deception will become so intense that they will make idols of the symbols used in worship, worshiping what they themselves have created and leading others to do the same. This false worship pervades all walks of life, rich and poor, free and slave, educated and untaught. No one can escape the influence of the beast except with the truth that comes only from God.

This last beast becomes so powerful that he marks people with a mark. Those without his mark are oppressed by those who have been marked. Commerce is limited to those with the mark. Those without the mark are excluded. There are several cases in recent history where governments have required marks or papers or some proof of loyalty to live and do business within their borders. Without the proper identification, participation in the society is limited or not allowed. When religion and government are combined, people who fail to comply often face persecution. History is filled with stories where rulers gain control of the food supply and say, "Do it my way or don't eat." These societies or religions reflect the operation of the second beast and will appear and disappear throughout history.

The Mark of the Beast: Revelation 13:16–18

The mark of the beast is a specific number: 666. The number six falls short of the seven spirits of God and is the number ascribed to man. That number is repeated because there are countless religions invented by the minds of men and the craftiness of the devil. Being the prince of this world, Satan has charge of the world's resources and uses the desires of men to turn them away from the true God while maintaining the appearance of divine worship. "For men will be lovers of self, lovers of money, boastful, arrogant, revilers, disobedient to parents, ungrateful, unholy, unloving, irreconcilable, malicious gossips, without self-control, brutal, haters of good, treacherous, reckless, conceited, lovers of pleasure rather than lovers of God, holding to a form of godliness, although they have denied its power; Avoid such men as these" (2 Timothy 3:2–5). Just as men created idols during the days of Moses, people create religions that suit them during the days of Christ.

The two beasts represent the two strongest tests of Christian faith, worldliness, and false religion. The lure of the flesh, the first beast, is strong and brings with it temptation. "But each one is tempted when he is carried away and enticed by his own lust" (James 1:14). When we yield to temptation, we separate ourselves from God. That separation is called sin. When we worship that which is not God, the second beast, this too separates us from God and is also sin. This is Satan's purpose and desire— to separate us from God.

CHAPTER 14

THE BEGINNING OF
THE LAST DAYS

Where is Mount Zion? Is this a real mountain? Who are the 144,000? Is this an actual count of people? Where did they come from? What is the eternal Gospel? How does this Gospel differ from the little book? Has the war in heaven come to earth? Does everyone have to choose a side? Who are the reapers? What are they harvesting? Why does this harvest produce blood?

The Last Covenant: Revelation 14:1–5

Once again John's vision turns to heaven, and he sees Jesus standing on Mount Zion. With Him are 144,000 sealed with the seal of God and Jesus. These are the same 144,000 seen in chapter 7. They have been redeemed from the earth because of their faithfulness to God. They stand with Jesus because He now claims them as their risen Messiah. Described as chaste virgins, they have never followed idols or the way of the world but have remained loyal to God. They respected the truth and did not yield to the lies of the devil.

The song they sing cannot be learned because the way of their salvation is complete. Bought with the blood of the Lamb from the tribes of Israel, they now follow Christ. "So the dragon was enraged with the woman, and went off to make war with the rest of her children, who keep the commandments of God and hold to the testimony of Jesus" (Revelation 12:17). The law of Moses has served its purpose and the number of those saved under the law is complete. "Therefore the Law has become our tutor to lead us to Christ, so that we may be justified by faith" (Galatians 3:24). The 144,000 represent all those saved during the time of God's covenant with the twelve tribes of Israel, both Jew and Gentile. "For when Gentiles who do not have the Law do instinctively the things of the Law, these, not having the Law, are a law to themselves" (Romans 2:14).

The Gospel of Christ: Revelation 14:6–8

John now sees an angel flying through heaven carrying an eternal Gospel for every nation, tribe, tongue, and people. Good news for everyone who will listen. The message is simple: believe in Christ and give glory to God. This offer is prompted by the love of God. "For God so loved the world, that He gave His only begotten Son, that whoever believes in Him shall not perish, but have eternal life" (John 3:16). This Gospel is also eternal, which makes it the last offer from God.

Many people use the visions of John to make statements about the "last days." From the time this eternal Gospel is revealed to men until judgment day is indeed the last days. During these last days, the beast from the earth, the second beast, is distorting the truth about Jesus. Spouting lies and false teaching, this beast uses even these visions given to John to teach lies and lead people away from the truth.

The apostle Paul told the Galatians there was no other Gospel. "But even if we, or an angel from heaven, should preach to you a gospel contrary to what we have preached to you, he is to be accursed!" (Galatians 1:8). Peter said that there is salvation nowhere else. "And there is salvation in no one else; for there is no other name under heaven that has been given among men by which we must be saved" (Acts 4:12). It is only the pure teachings of Jesus that will lead us to truth and salvation.

This eternal Gospel is for every nation, tribe, and person. Jesus tells His apostles to go into all the world and preach this Gospel. "Go therefore and make disciples of all the nations, baptizing them in the name of the Father and the Son and the Holy Spirit, teaching them to observe all that I commanded you; and lo, I am with you always, even to the end of the age" (Matthew 28:19–20). Salvation is open to any and to all who will accept God's message and acknowledge Him as the Creator. It is a simple Gospel: fear God and give Him glory. No special buildings. No difficult laws. No designated sacrifices. A simple Gospel of love. Love God, and love your fellow man. Do unto others as you would have them do unto you. A simple Gospel that should be good news for everyone. A call to be born again, not of the flesh but of the spirit. A call to become a child of God!

Judgment: Revelation 14:8

A second angel follows the first, proclaiming the fall of Babylon. This is a warning to choose wisely. Accepting God's offer is salvation. Choosing the world, Babylon, is choosing that which is doomed to fail. The eternal Gospel brings salvation to men, but it also brings judgment for the people who refuse to heed the message of Christ. There will be those who will refuse God's offer. Those who refuse this final offer from God will find themselves without salvation. "For if we go on sinning willfully after receiving the knowledge of the truth, there no longer remains a sacrifice for sins, but a terrifying expectation of judgment and THE FURY OF A FIRE WHICH WILL CONSUME THE ADVERSARIES" (Hebrews 10:26–27). It is for these people that the second angel cries, "Fallen, fallen, fallen is Babylon the great." Trusting in the world and the teaching of men will result in their destruction. People who fall prey to the beasts of the dragon and surrender their souls to the world will share the fate of fallen Babylon.

Babylon: Revelation 14:8

Led by Nebuchadnezzar, whose power came from God, the nation of Babylon captured Jerusalem in 597 BC. "Now on the seventh day of the fifth month, which was the nineteenth year of King Nebuchadnezzar, king of Babylon, Nebuzaradan the captain of the guard, a servant of the king of Babylon, came to Jerusalem. He burned the house of the Lord, the king's house, and all the houses of Jerusalem; even every great house he burned with fire" (2 Kings 25:8–9). When Jerusalem fell, the remnant of God's people were carried off into captivity.

It seemed that the nation of Israel had come to an end, having been swallowed up by the most powerful nation the world had ever seen. Faith in God survived amid the decadence of Babylon. Daniel and others kept faith with God, not surrendering to the riches and pleasures offered by the world. Babylon became a symbol of the sin that so easily entangles us. Babylon is described as a woman who has captured all the nations with her immorality just as an immoral woman can lure men off the proper path with a promise of momentary pleasure.

Babylon is the enemy of God's chosen and the oppressor of all who seek a life in an eternal realm outside of this world. Babylon represents the world and the things in the world ruled by that great dragon of old, Satan. Just as Satan rules this Babylon, Nebuchadnezzar ruled the Babylon of Israel's captivity. Just as God was in control of Nebuchadnezzar's power, God is in control of Satan's power. "While the word was in the king's mouth, a voice came from heaven, saying, 'King Nebuchadnezzar, to you it is declared: sovereignty has been removed from you'" (Daniel 4:31).

Doom for Satan's Followers: Revelation 14:9–11

A third angel proclaims doom to those who worship the beast and carry his mark. (Choosing to follow a false religion is following the beast.) When Christ and His Gospel enter the world, Satan is doomed. Death has been conquered with the resurrection of Jesus. The fear of death, Satan's best weapon, is conquered with the preaching of the Gospel. "Therefore, since the children share in flesh and blood, He Himself likewise also partook of the same, that through death He might render powerless him who had the power of death, that is, the devil, and might free those who through fear of death were subject to slavery all their lives" (Hebrews 2:14–15).

People who do not believe the Gospel and follow the teachings of Christ are aligned with Satan and are condemned with him. Their fate is cast with the beast and will last forever and ever. The righteousness and love of God overpowers the evil of Satan. The followers of Jesus will turn their backs on the pleasures of this world just as Moses did. "By faith Moses, when he had grown up, refused to be called the son of Pharaoh's daughter, choosing rather to endure ill-treatment with the people of God than to enjoy the passing pleasures of sin" (Hebrews 11:24–25).

The followers of Jesus seek a better world. A city not made with hands. Because the world has no sway over them, they are persecuted and killed, but death has been defeated by Jesus and their faith protects them from the lure of the world, the fear of death and the fate of the devil.

This judgment and doom are created by the proclaiming of the Gospel. People will find that they are on one side or the other. This is the sword Jesus promised. The eternal Gospel is the sword spoken of by the writer of Hebrews—the sword that can separate the soul from the spirit. "For the word of God is living and active and sharper than any two-edged sword, and piercing as far as the division of soul and spirit, of both joints and marrow, and able to judge the thoughts and intentions of the heart" (Hebrews 4:12). This is the start of a process that will continue until the end of time itself.

The Dead Who Die in Christ: Revelation 14:12–13

Just as doom is proclaimed on those who are loyal to the dragon, redemption and rest are proclaimed for those who trust in Christ. They are promised that death is only a peaceful interlude. A promise from a God who cannot lie. "In the same way God, desiring even more to show to the heirs of the promise the unchangeableness of His purpose, interposed with an oath, so that by two unchangeable things in which it is impossible for God to lie, we who have taken refuge would have strong encouragement to take hold of the hope set before us. This hope we have as an anchor of the soul, a hope both sure and steadfast and one which enters within the veil" (Hebrews 6:17–19).

The Reapers: Revelation 14:14–16

John sees a white cloud and someone sitting on the cloud, "one like the son of man." This son of man had a golden crown on his head and a sickle in his hand. The crown shows authority, and the sickle shows preparation and purpose. The reaping begins with a command brought from the temple where God the Father dwells. God Himself has decreed that it is time for the harvest.

When the Gospel of Jesus is preached, the harvest begins. The apostles are told in Samaria that the fields are "ripe with the harvest." "Do you not say, 'There are yet four months, and then comes the harvest'? Behold, I say to you, lift up your eyes and look on the fields, that they are white for harvest" (John 4:35). The eternal Gospel of Jesus is reaping souls everywhere it is being preached.

The Second Reaper: Revelation 14:17–20

A second reaper with a second sickle appears from within the temple. The second reaper is given the command to reap by an angel that has authority over fire or burning. This second reaper gathers the grapes that are to be trodden under foot. The juice from that trampling is likened unto blood and flows forth in a great stream. The prophet Joel uses similar language and blames their trampling on their own great wickedness. "Put in the sickle, for the harvest is ripe. Come, tread, for the wine press is full; The vats overflow, for their wickedness is great" (Joel 3:13). Two harvests, two fates, brought about because the Gospel is being proclaimed in all the earth. When the reaping begins, it will be glorious for some, but for others, it will be the greatest of dooms.

CHAPTER 15

A SCENE IN HEAVEN

Why are there seven angels? What are the seven plagues? Why is God's wrath described as plagues? Why are some separated from the plagues?

The Seven Angels: Revelation 15:1

Seven angels appear with seven plagues: messengers from God carrying the doom of those who have rejected His Son, Jesus Christ. The fate of all those who come after the Gospel message is preached is based on the acceptance or rejection of Jesus. A plague is not a sudden and quick death but an illness, often drawn out and painful, that results in the death of large numbers of people. A plague is said to "run its course," meaning that a length of time is involved. The seven plagues of God are active during the same period of time as the preaching of the Gospel.

Those Separated from the Plagues: Revelation 15:2–4

On the sea of glass mixed with fire appear those who have conquered the temptations of the two beasts and have held true to the teachings of

God's lamb. They are now here before the throne of God, protected from the seven plagues that God is about to unleash on the world. They proclaim the glory of God and their faith in Him with a song and harps provided by God Himself. These are the ones who throughout the ages follow God's teaching no matter the difficulty. They are separated from the plagues that are poured out upon the world. Their joy is not in the things of the world, but their joy is in praising God.

These are men, such as Moses and Stephen, who give their lives in service to God. Moses spent his long years in God's service and Steven died at the hands of rebellious men proclaiming his faith in Jesus. There are countless others, some named in the book of Hebrews and others who will come after the writing of the scriptures was completed. They stretch from the beginning of God's great plan until its completion. They stand above the sea that is mixed with the fire of God's wrath unharmed by the seven plagues released upon the rest of the world.

The Seven Plagues: Revelation 15:5–8

After confirming the safety of God's faithful, the visions turn to the destruction of the seven plagues. There are seven angels, seven bowls, and seven plagues. Seven because they come from the presence of God. They come from the temple of testimony or witness. They are a part of the Gospel message that is being preached. They are a witness or testimony of the power and presence of God in our world. (The sun can warm us and give us light or scorch our skin and blind us when we do not respect its power.)

The seven angels are clean and bright and do the bidding of God. They carry the bowls out of the temple of testimony where they can be poured out. These angels, servants of God, are dressed in clean, white linen and their waists are girded with gold sashes. The role they play in God's plan is one of honor. The bowls they carry and empty are a vital part of redemption because they contain the wrath of God. His wrath is contained and controlled.

This is not a fit of temper or a burst of anger but is a necessary part of the plan that redeems people from their sins. Some, like Jonah, need hard lessons to bring about repentance and obedience. These plagues are a last chance to repent and join the saints who have forsaken the treasures of the world and to sing with them on the sea of glass praising God. The plagues are part of God's great plan for the people He has created and is molding into a holy nation and a royal priesthood. "But you are A CHOSEN RACE, A royal PRIESTHOOD, A HOLY NATION, A PEOPLE FOR God's OWN POSSESSION, so that you may proclaim the excellencies of Him who has called you out of darkness into His marvelous light" (1 Peter 2:9). They come to those who will not repent and seek God.

CHAPTER 16

POURING OUT GOD'S WRATH

Why is God pouring out wrath on the earth? Why is the last bowl called Armageddon? Why does each bowl attack a different aspect of creation? How do these plagues show God's power over creation?

The Six Bowls of Wrath: Revelation 16:1–12

When John sees the bowls poured out, each one strikes a different aspect of creation, each part is infected with a plague, and no part is left out. The malignant sores and the foulness of the water may not be seen by the people inhabiting the earth, but from God's throne, the destruction is clearly visible, and the results will soon be seen by all. Sin, which has infested the world since the days of Adam, has a visible and an invisible effect on creation. We see the results of sin as it is manifested in our physical world. God sees all the effects of sin.

The First Plague: Revelation 16:2

The first plague infects the flesh of all who bear the mark of the beast, that "number" from chapter 13 that marks men as serving religion and not God. People, having itching ears, are quick to take up any teaching that gives them comfort, not knowing or not caring that it does nothing to reconcile them to God. "For the time will come when they will not endure sound doctrine; but wanting to have their ears tickled, they will accumulate for themselves teachers in accordance to their own desires" (2 Timothy 4:3).

As more and more people populate the earth, there are more and more false teachers. Only a sincere search for God's truth will find the Gospel. People infected by this first plague find the Gospel a source of constant pain and irritation. They find no peace in false teaching but will not yield to the truth. Their souls suffer in the same way as the flesh of Job suffered from boils "Then Satan went out from the presence of the LORD and smote Job with sore boils from the sole of his foot to the crown of his head. And he took a potsherd to scrape himself while he was sitting among the ashes" (Job 2:7–8).

The Second Plague: Revelation 16:3

The largest body of water, the sea, is turned into blood by the second bowl. There will be no more life-giving food from the sea. It is not even fit for travel. The sea that God created on the third day and filled with life will no longer serve humankind. The terror of the sea should have men reaching out in prayer to the God that can save them.

The Third Plague: Revelation 16:4–7

Next struck is the fresh water necessary for life. Nowhere is there fresh water for quenching thirst and sustaining life. Jesus brought the living water into the world, and the fresh waters of creation are no longer sufficient for life. "He who believes in Me, as the Scripture said, 'From his innermost being will flow rivers of living water'" (John 7:38).

The angel pouring out this bowl also pours forth praise to God for His judgment. Because the unrepentant of the world have shed the blood of the righteous, they will never quench their thirst. The Gospel they reject is the source of the living water they need to live. All of heaven joins with the angel praising God for this judgment.

The Fourth Plague: Revelation 16:8–9

The fourth angel pours out the plague upon the sun. The source of God's light becomes a torment to those who refuse to accept God's glory. Just as the unbelieving people lost all reason and turned in anguish on Stephen, the truth will be a source of agony throughout time for those who do not want or accept God's Gospel plan of salvation. "Now when they heard this, they were cut to the quick, and they began gnashing their teeth at him" (Acts 7:54). Overpowered by God's glory, their souls burn and suffer. They lash out at the only thing that can relieve their pain: the Gospel. Even in their agony, they refuse to repent and acknowledge God. Denying the only source of salvation, they are doomed.

The first four plagues repeat the destruction described at the sounding of the first four trumpets. The introduction of the eternal Gospel does not remove sin from the earth but does offer a way to escape. The physical world where we live has not changed with the sacrifice of Christ. The resurrection of Christ opens a door from our world into the presence of God. Jesus is that door. "Jesus answered, 'I am the way and the truth and the life. No one comes to the Father except through me'" (John 14:6).

The Fifth Plague: Revelation 16:10–11

Satan is not excluded from these plagues. The fifth angel pours out God's wrath on Satan's throne. When Christ conquers death, Satan's power is greatly diminished. People become free from the fear of dying and turn in multitudes to God. "Therefore, since the children share in flesh and blood, He Himself likewise also partook of the same, that through death He might render powerless him who had the power of death, that is, the devil, and might free those who through fear of death were subject to slavery all their lives" (Hebrews 2:14–15). Satan's kingdom is darkened, and his rule is over.

For many he is no longer the prince of the earth, and his promises of worldly treasure and power are rubbish compared to the promise of eternal life. People he once controlled, like Paul the apostle, are set free by Jesus. "But whatever things were gain to me, those things I have counted as loss for the sake of Christ. More than that, I count all things to be loss in view of the surpassing value of knowing Christ Jesus my Lord, for whom I have suffered the loss of all things, and count them but rubbish so that I may gain Christ" (Philippians 3:7–8).

People still under Satan's control blaspheme, blaming their troubles on God and not on the rejection of His saving message. Clinging to the deeds that separate them from God and salvation, they refuse God's message and will not repent. "But realize this, that in the last days difficult times will come. For men will be lovers of self, lovers of money, boastful, arrogant, revilers, disobedient to parents, ungrateful, unholy, unloving, irreconcilable, malicious gossips, without self-control, brutal, haters of good, treacherous, reckless, conceited, lovers of pleasure rather than lovers of God, holding to a form of godliness, although they have denied its power; Avoid such men as these" (2 Timothy 3:1–5).

The Sixth Plague: Revelation 16:12

The Euphrates is one of the four rivers that flows out of Eden. It has been named on several occasions in scripture as a boundary for the land of God's people. A boundary where enemies were stopped and a boundary where the invasion began. When the sixth bowl is poured out, the Euphrates dries up and is no longer a barrier to destruction. This opens the door for the kings of the east who bring destruction as described in chapter 9.

Even when faced with these terrifying times, there are people who will refuse to repent. "The rest of mankind, who were not killed by these plagues, did not repent of the works of their hands, so as not to worship demons, and the idols of gold and of silver and of brass and of stone and of wood, which can neither see nor hear nor walk; and they did not repent of their murders nor of their sorceries nor of their immorality nor of their thefts" (Revelation 9:20–21).

Armageddon: Revelation 16:13–16

From Satan the father of lies comes three spirits looking like frogs. They represent the first beast which appeals to the desires of the flesh, the second beast and the false prophet which deceive men into following false doctrine. They come to gather the wicked of humankind into a battle against God. Using lies, deceit, and lust, these unseen spirits will align people with the devil. People who love the world will use their resources and their lives to war against God and His message of salvation. "For the mind set on the flesh is death, but the mind set on the Spirit is life and peace, because the mind set on the flesh is hostile toward God; for it does not subject itself to the law of God, for it is not even able to do so, and those who are in the flesh cannot please God" (Romans 8:6–8). This is the often discussed battle of Armageddon.

Armageddon is often described as an actual battle that will take place between the forces of good and evil. The battle between the forces of good and the forces of evil is being fought each and every day. When the Gospel is preached and heard, conflict begins: believe or not believe and obey or disobey. That battle can even be fought within our very selves. "I find then the principle that evil is present in me, the one who wants to do good. For I joyfully concur with the law of God in the inner man, but I see a different law in the members of my body, waging war against the law of my mind and making me a prisoner of the law of sin which is in my members" (Romans 7:21–23). Paul continues, stating, "Who will set me free." Paul continues by giving his thanks to God for Jesus Christ, who sets us free from sin and death. "Therefore there is now no condemnation for those who are in Christ Jesus" (Romans 8:1). Those who are baptized into Christ escape the terror of the plagues poured from the bowls of wrath.

The Seventh Plague: Revelation 16:17–21

The seventh bowl of wrath is poured out on the air, and a loud voice speaking with the authority of God declares, "It is done." At the beginning of this vision (Revelation 15:1), before the angels with the bowls of wrath are released to pour out the plagues, there is a vision of the victorious standing on the sea of glass singing praises to Moses and the Lamb. They are spared the destruction of the plagues that are falling on the unbelievers and disobedient.

"And you were dead in your trespasses and sins, in which you formerly walked according to the course of this world, according to the prince of the power of the air, of the spirit that is now working in the sons of disobedience. Among them we too all formerly lived in the lusts of our flesh, indulging the desires of the flesh and of the mind, and were by nature children of wrath, even as the rest. But God, being rich in mercy, because of His great love with which He loved us, even when we were dead in our transgressions, made us alive together with Christ (by grace you have been saved), and raised us up with Him, and seated us with Him in the heavenly places in Christ Jesus" (Ephesians 2:1–6).

With the last plague come thunder and lighting and earthquakes such as have never been seen. After the ungodly have rejected and killed God's Son, they continue to reject His message of repentance and salvation. There remains no salvation left for them. "For if we go on sinning willfully after receiving the knowledge of the truth, there no longer remains a sacrifice for sins, but a terrifying expectation of judgment and THE FURY OF A FIRE WHICH WILL CONSUME THE ADVERSARIES" (Hebrews 10:26–27).

The great city (Babylon) was split into three parts, each led away from God by one of the three deceiving spirits. The lust of the flesh, the lust of the eyes, and the pride of life together are called Babylon. That great city of old that held God's people in captivity represents all the decadence and wealth of the world that lure people away from the love of God. "Do not love the world nor the things in the world. If anyone loves the world, the love of the Father is not in him. For all that is in the world, the lust of the flesh and the lust of the eyes and the boastful pride of life, is not from the Father, but is from the world. The world is passing away, and also its lusts; but the one who does the will of God lives forever" (1 John 2:15–17).

The mountains and islands flee, and Babylon is struck with severe hail. There is no place to hide from God's wrath and men rail against God because their chosen way of life is fleeting and unsatisfying. Their fate has been sealed because they love the world more than they love God. The lovers of the world cry in distress because all that they love is being destroyed. They rebel and refuse to yield to the righteousness of God. The wrath that comes upon them they have brought on themselves by not accepting God's message of salvation. They reap what they have sown. "Do not be deceived, God is not mocked; for whatever a man sows, this he will also reap. For the one who sows to his own flesh will from the flesh reap corruption, but the one who sows to the Spirit will from the Spirit reap eternal life" (Galatians 6:7–8).

CHAPTER 17

THE WORLD IS JUDGED

Who or what is Babylon? Why does the last bowl need more explanation? What is the beast? What do the seven mountains mean? Are the seven kings certain rulers from history or the future? What are the many waters?

Babylon: Revelation 17:1–6

The angel who had poured out the seventh bowl came to John in his vision and explained the destruction of Babylon. The angel compares Babylon to a harlot or prostitute giving herself to any man who asks or pays but with loyalty to none. Not everyone can possess her, but all can lust after her. That lust will by itself become sin and separate a soul from God. "But I say to you that everyone who looks at a woman with lust for her has already committed adultery with her in his heart" (Matthew 5:28).

Those who lust after the riches and pleasures of the world (Babylon) set their souls in opposition to God. Their opposition to God causes them to persecute and even kill those that worship God. The rulers of the world have forsaken God in their lust for her. Others act like people who are drunk, having lost their inhibitions and reason because of longing after her.

The Mystery Explained: Revelation 17:7

The vision shifts to a wilderness where John sees a woman covered in the treasures of the world sitting on a scarlet beast. The beast is the same beast seen coming out of the sea in chapter 13 having seven heads and ten horns and filled with vileness. This beast is given authority throughout the earth so that he may war against the followers of Jesus. The woman riding on the beast is adorned in purple and scarlet while wearing the riches of the world and holding in her hand a golden cup filled with abominations and evil.

The name on her forehead is Babylon, the city that captured and carried off God's chosen people and the symbol of decadence and worldly power. Unfaithful, with no loyalty or respect, concerned only with herself, Babylon (the riches and pleasures of the world) has lured generations of men to their destruction. The lure of wealth, fame, or power has turned many a person away from serving God or has captured their eyes in a manner that kept them from even seeing God. Throughout time, men of God have been despised and even killed by those chasing worldliness. A harlot drunk with the blood of the saints is an excellent picture to describe worldliness. When John sees her, he is mystified and impressed by her. This is a vision that needs to be understood, and the angel sets out to explain it to John.

The Beast: Revelation 17:8

The beast is described in what may seem like confusing terms, but remember the angel is explaining the mystery to John and intends for John and the reader to understand the message of the vision. The first description of the beast is one of time. The beast was and is not and is about to come out of the abyss and go to destruction. Satan is immortal. He works through all of God's creation and throughout time to lie and deceive.

The false promises of the world's pleasures have been here since creation and have been used by the devil to deceive and destroy since time began. Once the dragon was in heaven, then he was not. "Then another sign appeared in heaven: and behold, a great red dragon having seven heads and ten horns, and on his heads were seven diadems. And his tail swept away a third of the stars of heaven and threw them to the earth. And the dragon stood before the woman who was about to give birth, so that when she gave birth, he might devour her child" (Revelation 12:3–4). Soon he will be summoned back to face the wrath of God, and then he will be cast into the lake of fire prepared for him and his angels. "Then He will also say to those on His left, 'Depart from Me, accursed ones, into the eternal fire which has been prepared for the devil and his angels'" (Matthew 25:41).

The Seven Heads: Revelation 17:9–11

The seven heads become seven mountains that support the harlot who seduces the disobedient with the desires of the world. She is supported, sustained, and guided by the beast to carry out her atrocities against the saints. Her power and authority come from the deception of the beast, causing people to worship the beast instead of the holy God. The heads of the beast are also described as kings. There are five fallen kings no longer able to support the harlot in her immorality.

The advent of God's teaching in the world has caused many of Satan's myths and lies to be exposed. Knowledge from the teaching of God has filtered throughout the world despite the devil's best efforts. For example, idols are no longer made of stone and metal. Instead, people worship as idols false religions, ideals, or even humankind itself (humanism). Ignorance is no longer winked at, but men are called on everywhere to repent. God's message of salvation, the Gospel, is preached to every nation and people, leaving them without an excuse for remaining in sin. "Therefore having overlooked the times of ignorance, God is now declaring to men that all people everywhere should repent" (Acts 17:30).

This sixth king represents the changing tactics of Satan. He does not give up; he changes his schemes and lies to fit the times and places where he is lurking. This king represents the way the devil presents the treasures of the world in the last days. Modernism, humanism, and other modern philosophies have replaced false gods of the past. Men consider themselves too knowledgeable to fall for the legends and myths of the past. Instead, they fall for the same deceptions of the devil dressed in modern rhetoric. Worship and respect for God are replaced by science and nature. No matter how it is worded or painted, if it is not God's truth, it is a lie and a deception from the devil that will lead to destruction.

The last king is yet to come. Satan has not exhausted his efforts to overthrow God. He will continue the war he began in heaven. New lies will be told, and new deceptions will be created for as long as the world exists. The lure of the world will be presented as desirable for as long as the devil remains prince of the air.

Though unseen, the true head of the beast has always been there, the eighth head. Hidden, he is the devil himself. Described in John's earlier visions as a head that was slain yet alive, he mimics the Gospel message of the resurrection of Christ without the power to impart life. His followers, both human and spirit, oppose God. Following the teaching of false prophets and chasing the desires of the flesh has caused them to worship the beast instead of God. They give power to the harlot by becoming a part of the persecution and killing of the saints.

The Ten Horns: Revelation 17:12–13

John is told the ten horns are ten kings, rulers that are a part of the beast and add to the power of the harlot (Babylon). For a short time, they will appear to rule, but they have no authority because they are subject to the will of the beast. The number ten is the number of completeness (man six and earth four). These kings are all the rulers on earth who serve the beast and worship the harlot. Because they receive their authority from the beast, they have no true authority.

Such kings have come and gone through the ages. Some kings ruled before John saw these visions, and some kings will rule after. Such rulers will come and go until God completes His wrath. The number ten means there will be such kings until the world (Babylon) has ended. This vision depicts that ending.

The War: Revelation 17:14

All these things war against the teachings of the Lamb. Love your neighbor as yourself does not work side by side with the lust for power, fame, and riches. Those engaged in the pursuit of the lust of the flesh, the lust of the eyes, and the pride of life are in a constant struggle with each other. They cannot win because the methods they use in their war are self-defeating and because they war against the ultimate authority and power. Christ will not rejoice in His victory alone because those who believe in His name (accept His authority) and follow Him will share the victory with Him.

The Many Waters: Revelation 17:15

The many waters that the harlot is first seen sitting upon represent the many divisions of the people of the earth. Any division among people, whether it is physical barriers (natural or created), culture, language, or color that promotes strife, serves the beast and feeds the harlot (Babylon) on his back. Godless people will chase the harlot looking for satisfaction and pleasure that is not there.

They will hate her for controlling their lives without giving them the satisfaction they seek. Strife will destroy the very things they lust for. The world's pleasures are temporary and are consumed by their use. Godless people serve God's plan and purpose even as they struggle to disobey Him. Conflict brings strength to the faith of those who believe and trust in God's Son. They are accomplishing His will while denying His authority.

CHAPTER 18

WORLDLINESS IS DOOMED

Why has Babylon fallen? What makes Babylon so bad? Why does God call for people to come out of Babylon? Why does Babylon hold such an attraction for some people? Is there no hope for Babylon?

Babylon Has Fallen: Revelation 18:1–3

"Fallen. Fallen is Babylon the great," cries the angel with great authority. As the day of the Lord approaches, the doom of the sinful world draws near. Her fate is sealed by her own deeds. Babylon has become a home for demons and unclean spirits and the foul birds that fed upon death and corruption. Having become repulsive to God, she has caused her own destruction. The corrupt world we live in cannot endure the presence of God in His heavenly form. When Jesus returns, the wickedness of the world will bring about its own destruction.

Babylon's wickedness is shared by every nation on earth throughout all the existence of earth. There is not a generation of man that has not participated in chasing wealth and immorality, persecuting the righteous in the process. The harlot is not one single city or nation but is all the people who have devoted their lives to pursuits contrary to God's plan for man. People in their pride have forsaken their true God for visions of power and fame. Others, lusting with their eyes, have pursued the glittering trinkets of earthly wealth, ignoring the true riches of God. Many have even worshiped the corrupt flesh and its pleasures at the expense of their souls.

God Calls His People from the World: Revelation 18:4–8

A voice calls from heaven to those loyal to God to come out of the evil of Babylon. Just as God called His people out of a physical Egypt during the days of Moses, His Gospel message is calling people to leave sin and worldliness behind and to be holy. "As obedient children, do not be conformed to the former lusts which were yours in your ignorance, but like the Holy One who called you, be holy yourselves also in all your behavior; because it is written, 'YOU SHALL BE HOLY, FOR I AM HOLY'" (1 Peter 1:14–16). Those who continue to love and follow the harlot Babylon will suffer the fate of Babylon.

Leaving Babylon is not a physical departure from the world but a rejection of the world's temptations and a turning to the spiritual teachings of God. "I have given them Your word; and the world has hated them, because they are not of the world, even as I am not of the world. I do not ask You to take them out of the world, but to keep them from the evil one. They are not of the world, even as I am not of the world" (John 17:14–16). The people of God will not suffer with those who have brought God's wrath upon themselves.

The punishment that falls upon the world will not be held back. The pride and power of the world will be as nothing before the awesome strength of the Lord. Those who lusted after her riches and glory will mourn her demise. Her destruction is the inevitable outcome of her nature. Riches perish with the using and power shifts from those who grow weak to those who are for a short time strong.

The Lament for Babylon: Revelation 18:9–20

Even as the great city is laid waste, those who love her have eyes for nothing else. They do not turn to God even in this moment of destruction proving God's justice and solidifying their choice of evil over good. With the world gone, where will they dwell? Not with God. They are unworthy, not wanting what has been offered. If allowed, they would remake the evil they desire. The evil that is described as Babylon the harlot. All the righteous killed by "lovers of the world" are receiving the justice long prayed for and awaited.

The Millstone: Revelation 18:21–24

An angel casts a millstone into the sea to illustrate the complete end of the devil's kingdom. When the stone sinks, it is gone forever, leaving no trace of its existence. When the world we know ceases, it will not come back. Where will those who place their faith and hope in the world live? They cannot live with the saints they mocked, oppressed, and persecuted. There will remain only a furnace of fire where there will be weeping and gnashing of teeth. "So just as the tares are gathered up and burned with fire, so shall it be at the end of the age. The Son of Man will send forth His angels, and they will gather out of His kingdom all stumbling blocks, and those who commit lawlessness, and will throw them into the furnace of fire; in that place there will be weeping and gnashing of teeth" (Matthew 13:40–42).

CHAPTER 19

HEAVEN REJOICES

Why is there joy in heaven? Who does the rejoicing? Who is the Lamb? Who does He marry? When in time does this marriage take place?

The Four Hallelujahs: Revelation 19:1–6

The destruction of Babylon and the gathering of God's people bring great rejoicing in heaven. Four hallelujahs ring throughout the home of God. The first and second hallelujahs are shouted by a great unseen multitude in heaven. Those who rejoice when a sinner comes to repentance will also rejoice and give praise to God when His salvation is complete. "In the same way, I tell you, there is joy in the presence of the angels of God over one sinner who repents" (Luke 15:10). They have watched as God's plan of salvation has unfolded. They have witnessed the persecution of His prophets and the death of His Son. Now they shout hallelujah as they witness the justice of God. The light of the Gospel has illuminated the defilement of the world.

They shout a second hallelujah because the corruption and defilements of the world can no longer entangle men's souls. There will be no more persecution of God's people. There will be no more trials and temptations of the saints of God.

The third hallelujah comes from the twenty-four elders and the four living creatures who are constantly before God's throne. Amen and hallelujah because God has accomplished the separation of good from evil. Amen and hallelujah because only God could accomplish this separation. Being the closest to God, they are filled with joy at this great deed. A voice from the throne calls for praise from all of God's followers proclaiming His authority and might.

Then a great multitude rings forth with praise for God. These voices are rejoicing for the people who were rescued by their God from sin and the corrupt world where they lived. A world filled with sin and death described as a great harlot. Truly an awesome God and worthy of our respect and praise. Who else could have redeemed the good from among the evil? Heaven is transformed into an even greater place of rejoicing than it was before.

The mighty voice of the great multitude and all of heaven continues its praise of God, declaring the marriage of the lamb. Jesus is the Lamb and the bride is the church. "Husbands, love your wives, just as Christ also loved the church and gave Himself up for her, so that He might sanctify her, having cleansed her by the washing of water with the word, that He might present to Himself the church in all her glory, having no spot or wrinkle or any such thing; but that she would be holy and blameless" (Ephesians 5:25–27). Just as a bride is clothed in her finest, the church is clothed in the righteous acts of the saints. The groom only sees the beauty of the bride, never her weaknesses. The long-awaited day that unites the followers of Jesus with their Savior has come.

The Marriage of the Lamb: Revelation 19:7–9

The angel speaks to John commanding him to write of the great blessing it is to be invited to the marriage feast of the Lamb. When Babylon is destroyed, the bride of Christ, the church, will be united with Jesus for eternity. There will be rejoicing in heaven much like the joy of a wedding feast. Jesus often taught parables about a marriage feast. Jesus spoke of people who were invited and made excuses of why they could not come. Jesus spoke of those who would attend but were unprepared. Jesus even taught about a man who was there but not dressed in the proper clothes and was cast out. A marriage is a special occasion of celebration whereby family and friends are invited and no one wants to see disharmony. Those on the guest list are carefully chosen and are people who will bring joy to the celebration.

The uniting of Jesus with His church is indeed a special occasion whereby there will only be those in attendance who bring joy to the celebration. No one else will be allowed. Indeed, it is a blessing and a privilege to attend.

A Fellow Servant: Revelation 19:10

John, overwhelmed with the magnificence of the occasion, falls to worship the angel. He is told, "Do not do that; I am a fellow servant of yours and your brethren who hold the testimony of Jesus." The saints of God, the bride of Christ, will be as much a part of heaven as the angels. We are not slaves but sons! "Because you are sons, God has sent forth the Spirit of His Son into our hearts, crying, 'Abba! Father!' Therefore you are no longer a slave, but a son; and if a son, then an heir through God" (Galatians 4:6–7). Sons who will live in God's house are honored as sons.

The Conqueror: Revelation 19:11–19

A new vision starts, a new message. Those who do not follow Christ will see not a groom who loves them but a conqueror who will defeat them. The description can only be Jesus. Faithful and true, the Word of God with authority like no other, He will be a fearful sight to those who have rejected His sacrifice. "How much severer punishment do you think he will deserve who has trampled under foot the Son of God, and has regarded as unclean the blood of the covenant by which he was sanctified, and has insulted the Spirit of grace?" (Hebrews 10:29).

He rides a white horse, the symbol of a successful conqueror. He is crowned with authority (diadems) and has great authority of His own (the name no one knows except Himself). His eyes are too bright to look upon. And He is followed by a heavenly host also riding white horses. Christ is not just powerful, but He is also righteous and just in His conquest. He will conquer with the strength of love and truth.

From His mouth comes a sharp sword. The words of His teaching are judging the world in its wickedness. "He who rejects Me and does not receive My sayings, has one who judges him; the word I spoke is what will judge him at the last day" (John 12:48). His teaching destroys any excuse for believing the lies of Satan. His authority is absolute. The child attacked by the dragon (chapter 12) has returned for a day of reckoning. The King of Kings cannot be overruled.

An angel calls to the carrion birds to come to feast on the flesh of those who oppose Jesus. No matter their station, commanders, or mighty men, great or small, all who oppose Him will fall before Jesus. Even the spiritual *forces* of wickedness led by the beast cannot prevail. Christ is conquering them all with His Gospel of truth.

The Fall of the False Prophet: Revelation 19:20–21

Everywhere the Gospel of Christ is being preached. The beast (lust of the flesh) and the false prophet (man-made religion) are falling before the truth. The vision shows them seized and cast alive into the lake of fire. They have no power to destroy the people who follow the teaching of Jesus. All the people who follow the beast and accept his mark have their flesh given to the carrion birds. They are already dead in their sins. "And you were dead in your trespasses and sins, in which you formerly walked according to the course of this world, according to the prince of the power of the air, of the spirit that is now working in the sons of disobedience" (Ephesians 2:1–2).

Like a field after an ancient battle with swords and axes, the conquered are left in the field for the carron birds while the victors celebrate. There is no celebration for those lying in the field who have lost everything.

CHAPTER 20

THE FATE OF SATAN

Why is Satan bound? Is this the only time Satan was bound? Why one thousand years? Why is Satan set free? What is Satan's relationship to the Gospel of Christ? What is the first resurrection? What happens at the end of a thousand years?

The Thousand-Year Binding of Satan: Revelation 20:1–4

Satan is bound with a great chain and cast into an abyss for a thousand years. The Gospel truth is being preached throughout the world. With the truth available to everyone, Satan is no longer able to deceive the nations. All those who accept his lies for truth are without excuse. It will be this way for a period that is called a thousand years.

Time has no relevance in the realm where God lives. The thousand years signifies that Satan is bound until God's plan is complete. Satan was conquered and bound by God's authority when Jesus began His ministry.

This "thousand years" begins with the message of salvation from Jesus. No longer will Satan be able to deceive unwilling people because truth has come into the world. "So Jesus was saying to those Jews who had believed Him, 'If you continue in My word, then you are truly disciples of Mine;

Walking through Time with Jesus

and you will know the truth, and the truth will make you free'" (John 8:31–32). Jesus has brought a message of salvation and truth to everyone in every nation who will listen.

The casting out of Satan's demons was a display of the greater power of God. "But if I cast out demons by the Spirit of God, then the kingdom of God has come upon you. Or how can anyone enter the strong man's house and carry off his property, unless he first binds the strong man? And then he will plunder his house" (Matthew 12:28–29). Jesus's power over the devil was demonstrated each time He cast demons out and forbade them to speak of who He was.

He passed this power to His apostles. Demons cannot stand against the power of God that came into the world with the good news taught by Jesus and His followers. The conqueror on the white horse will defeat them all with the words from His mouth.

Satan's strongest effort to defeat the eternal Gospel manifested in the only begotten Son of God, Jesus, was made at the cross. He arrayed the forces of sin against the sinless Christ and brought Him to the cross. The crucifixion was intended not only to kill the messenger of God but also to silence the message. Satan planned for the disgrace and death of Jesus to prove untrue all the things Jesus taught. The golden rule (based in love) would be shown to have no power in a ruthless world.

When Jesus rose from the dead, His words of truth became more powerful than before. Good triumphed over evil. Righteousness triumphed over wickedness and death. Truth conquered lies. Satan is not yet destroyed, but his power is limited to the world, the abyss in which he lives. He can no longer deceive the nations because the Gospel (truth) has been made available to all men everywhere. "If indeed you continue in the faith firmly established and steadfast, and not moved away from the hope of the Gospel that you have heard, which was proclaimed in all creation under heaven, and of which I, Paul, was made a minister" (Colossians 1:23).

During the same thousand years, the period from the conquest of Satan until his judgment, the followers of Christ will reign with Him. The authority of Jesus, passed to the apostles, will continue throughout the ages to pass from generation to generation in the Gospel. His followers will reign with Him. "Behold, I stand at the door and knock; if anyone hears My voice and opens the door, I will come in to him and will dine

— 89 —

with him, and he with Me. He who overcomes, I will grant to him to sit down with Me on My throne, as I also overcame and sat down with My Father on His throne" (Revelation 3:20–21).

The First Resurrection: Revelation 20:5–6

The first resurrection is the life-giving blood of Jesus shared by all His followers. Because they believe, they will continue to live even after their bodies die. "Truly, truly, I say to you, if anyone keeps My word he will never see death" (John 8:51). "Jesus said to her, 'I am the resurrection and the life; he who believes in Me will live even if he dies, and everyone who lives and believes in Me will never die. Do you believe this?'" John 11:25–26). Those who do not believe are dead in their sin. They have forsaken the life offered in following Jesus and have no true life left in them. These will be returned from physical death to face judgment and exclusion from God's promise of peace and comfort for eternity.

Those not included in the redeemed of Jesus will face the second death. Judgment and condemnation for their continued refusal to yield to the truth is the second death. In short, this thousand-year period represents the last days in which we now live.

At the End of a Thousand Years: Revelation 20:7–10

When the thousand years are over, Satan will again be allowed all his power. He will gather with all his followers from the beginning of time and the power they bring. He will direct that power against Jesus Christ and His followers in a last effort to overcome and make himself supreme. He will lose. There is no great battle. The battle has already been fought and won by Jesus and His followers. "So the dragon was enraged with the woman, and went off to make war with the rest of her children, who keep the commandments of God and hold to the testimony of Jesus" (Revelation 12:17). Death and the fear of death, Satan's greatest weapons, have already been conquered. The power of God is so great that the army arrayed is simply devoured. Satan himself is cast into a lake of fire like so much chaff. His power compared to the conquering Christ is less than a child's.

His beast and false prophet are also cast into the lake of fire. This has been his destiny from the beginning. Just as God prepared a place for His saints, He prepared a place for those who wage war against Him. "Then He will also say to those on His left, 'Depart from Me, accursed ones, into the eternal fire which has been prepared for the devil and his angels'" (Matthew 25:41).

This is an eternal punishment just as heaven is an eternal reward. One will last just as long as the other. "These will go away into eternal punishment, but the righteous into eternal life" (Matthew 25:46). There will be no second war. Satan is doomed and those who follow him and the ways of the world are also doomed. God's plan has reached its final stage, the separation of all that is good from all that is evil. The righteous from the wicked. The godly from the ungodly. The holy from the unholy.

God the Father: Revelation 20:11–15

God appears seated upon a great white throne. His authority is seen in the throne, and His purity and justice are seen by its color. He has the right to make judgments, and there will be no mistakes.

Before Him are all the people of all time. No matter if they were kings and rulers or poor and little noticed by their companions, they will all stand before the throne of God. We will all stand before the throne of God.

There is a record of time written down. Nothing has been missed. All the works of each man are recorded so there can be no argument or denial. There will be no defense against the recorded evidence. Even the words we sometimes speak so carelessly are written there. "But I tell you that every careless word that people speak, they shall give an accounting for it in the day of judgment" (Matthew 12:36).

There is another book there called the book of life. In it are the names of those who have overcome sin. Not through their own works but through the blood of Jesus. This is a list of names of those washed in the blood of the Lamb. For them Jesus has already paid the price of sin. He stands here in place of those He has claimed as His own. An advocate for mercy. "My little children, I am writing these things to you so that you may not sin. And if anyone sins, we have an Advocate with the Father, Jesus Christ the righteous; and He Himself is the propitiation for our sins; and not for ours only, but also for those of the whole world" (1 John 2:1–2).

There is only judgment or mercy. Only those whose names are written in the book of life will receive mercy. All the others are cast with Satan into the lake of fire. This is the second death, eternal separation from God. Death and Hades are also cast into the lake of fire. There will be no more dying. "The last enemy that will be abolished is death" (1 Corinthians 15:26). Satan's power has been crushed and will never return. This is the third woe that was pronounced from heaven.

The first woe was for those who before the flood, left to their own free will, chose evil over good. The second woe was for those who, given law from God, could or would not live by that law. Law cannot make a man righteous. He will either follow the law and have no righteousness of his own or will fail to follow the law and will fall short of achieving righteousness from obedience. The third woe is for the people who reject the gift of salvation God has offered by sacrificing His only begotten Son. These are people who do not want good but desire evil. When offered a choice, they choose to serve evil and reject the love of God.

CHAPTER 21

A NEW PLACE TO LIVE

Why are these all things made new? Where are the old heaven and earth? Why is there a New Jerusalem? Who is the bride? Why is the new city founded upon the apostles? Why is the new city measured? Why is the city described using so many jewels?

The New Heaven and New Earth: Revelation 21:1–9

John sees a new world that he describes as a new heaven and a new earth. A place for God's people to dwell. The old earth and heaven are no more. "But the day of the Lord will come like a thief, in which the heavens will pass away with a roar and the elements will be destroyed with intense heat, and the earth and its works will be burned up" (2 Peter 3:10). Sin and corruption are no more. The people whose names are written in the book of life will have a fresh clean world in which to live. A world without corruption and sin. A world without dying or crying. A world without end.

The New Jerusalem: Revelation 21:10–14

John sees a New Jerusalem coming from God adorned as a bride. It too is fresh and new and ready for God and His people. No longer will there be restricted access to God, but He will Himself dwell among His people. God will wipe every tear from every eye. Death has been cast into the lake of fire and will not return.

The new world will be filled with joy. There will be no sorrow, no pain, no regrets. They have all passed away with the first world. And God declares that He has made "all things" new. John is instructed to write these words because they are as sure as God Himself. They are a message to God's people, a message that will outlast the rocks of earth and the stars of the sky. It is a message of hope and certainty that God will gather His people and they will dwell with Him in joy.

The message to John continues with the assurance from God that this will be an eternal home. The life-giving stream will not fail and will be free to all who dwell there. The people who dwell there will be loved as sons. Not everyone will be there. There will be no people there who disappoint and prey on others. The immoral and unbelievers along with idol worshippers and liars will have been cast into the lake of fire. This world is only for the righteous.

John is taken to a high mountain for a closer look at the New Jerusalem. He does not enter the city but is a witness to its beauty. Beautiful like a shining jewel or a bride adorned for her wedding, the city is beautiful. There are twelve gates and twelve foundations.

The gates are named after the tribes of Israel, and the foundations are named after the twelve apostles. This is a city of worship based on the teachings of the apostles about Jesus, including His crucifixion. "But we preach Christ crucified, to Jews a stumbling block and to Gentiles foolishness" (1 Corinthians 1:23). The teaching of the apostles is the foundation of this new city of worship.

The gates that open into the city came into existence because of the promises made to Abraham and his descendants. The original covenant given to the twelve tribes was a tutor to bring us to Christ. "Therefore the Law has become our tutor to lead us to Christ, so that we may be justified by faith" (Galatians 3:24). The entrance to worship of God and Christ is through Israel.

Christians are the adopted heirs of Abraham grafted into God's salvation. "And if you belong to Christ, then you are Abraham's descendants, heirs according to promise" (Galatians 3:29). "But if some of the branches were broken off, and you, being a wild olive, were grafted in among them and became partaker with them of the rich root of the olive tree" (Romans 11:17). The most important feature of the New Jerusalem is the missing temple. God and Christ dwell throughout the city. There is no need for priests and a meeting place because God and Christ are always there dwelling with the people.

Jerusalem Is Measured: Revelation 21:15–27

An angel is commanded to measure the city. It can be measured because it is complete. The walls define its completeness. The gates show its access. And the foundations describe its permanence. The city is so beautiful that it cannot be described in earthly terms. The size of the city is large enough to hold all its dwellers in comfort, and peace prevails within its walls. There is continuous light from the holiness of God. The gates are never closed because nothing evil and no dishonorable being will ever enter.

CHAPTER 22

A PICTURE OF THE HEAVEN TO COME

Why is there water in heaven? Where is the tree of life? Why is there no night? Jesus promises to return soon; is this promise made after judgment? Is this another shift in the time line of Revelation? What will be our relationship with the people who are serving God before we arrive in heaven?

The River of Life: Revelation 22:1–5

Within the city is the throne of God and of the Lamb. Coming from that throne is a river of life flowing down the street. The authority of God symbolized by the throne has given life as abundant as a river to all within the city. The tree of life from the days before sin is on each side of the river and is there for all its inhabitants, a group of people from all nations.

The curse from the garden is gone. The people of God are free from sin and death. They can serve God freely and with joy. There is no night. God's love and glory are their light. And there is no end. God's people will reign with Him forever. God is in their midst. There is joy beyond description!

The Return of Jesus: Revelation 22:6–7

Jesus says here, "I am coming soon." We are back to the present. Not limited to one moment in time, this invitation is repeated with each reading of the book of John's visions. Jesus has not yet returned, but His promise is sure and His return is certain. He pronounces a blessing on those who keep the prophecy of this book.

The words of prophecy spoken by God are not subject to the whims of men. Men can only heed them and bring themselves into harmony with God's plan. Just as in the past, the things God has promised will come about. There will be a new heaven and earth and a New Jerusalem. Accepting Jesus as the Son of God and keeping His commandments will assure our place within its walls.

Fellow Servants with the Angels: Revelation 22:8–9

When John falls to worship the angel, he is told not to worship the angel. The angel and John are fellow servants of God. So are the prophets and the believers of this book of visions. We are all servants of God, and each has a part to play in God's great plan of salvation. The body of Christ is made up of many members, each filling a role in salvation. "For just as we have many members in one body and all the members do not have the same function" (Romans 12:4).

This book of John's visions is not sent to change the behavior of unbelievers. The Gospel was sent for that purpose. This book of visions is sent to show the divine and eternal nature of Christ. The Alpha and the Omega that existed before creation, all through its existence, and after creation has opened the path of redemption for men everywhere. "For by Him all things were created, both in the heavens and on earth, visible and invisible, whether thrones or dominions or rulers or authorities—all things have been created through Him and for Him" (Colossians 1:16).

Jesus Christ has been active in creation from its first day and remains an active force in creation as long as it lasts. He is the triumphant conqueror who will conquer all His adversaries. Nothing can stand against Him, not even death. The words of this book are an assurance to those who accept

His words and follow Him that they will share in His triumph. Jesus says three times in the last scene of this book, "I am coming quickly."

He assures those who have listened to the Gospel and washed their robes in the blood of the Lamb that success will be theirs. Any cost for obedience will be seen as nothing compared to the reward. "But when this perishable will have put on the imperishable, and this mortal will have put on immortality, then will come about the saying that is written, 'Death is swallowed up in victory. O death, where is your victory? O death, where is your sting?'" (1 Corinthians 15:54–55).

Invitation and Warning: Revelation 22:10–21

The book ends with an invitation and a warning. All are invited. No one who is willing will be turned away. Some will hear and not want the reward offered. Some will find the path too hard or without immediate rewards. Some will not be willing to pay the cost of following Jesus. All are invited and all will respond, but not all will accept.

Those who hear the words of this book of visions are warned not to add or take away anything. There is no reason to add or remove anything from God's message. He says exactly what He intends to say. Any changes would be a rebellion against God.

The visions end with Jesus saying, "Yes, I come quickly." The writer is saying, "Amen. Come, Lord Jesus." "The grace of the Lord Jesus be with all, amen."

Appendix

The Rapture

The word *rapture* does not appear in John's book of visions. The basic concept of the rapture expresses the idea that when Jesus returns, only those who are believers will be resurrected. They will rule the earth in the air with Jesus for a thousand years. Those not taken up will be left on the earth. While this concept is very popular and has been the subject of many books and even a movie or two, I do not find this taught in the visions given to John. I have added this chapter to give you my thoughts about the resurrection of the saints.

Christ has promised a resurrection to those who believe in His name. "For this is the will of My Father, that everyone who beholds the Son and believes in Him will have eternal life, and I Myself will raise him up on the last day" (John 6:40).

Paul offers a vision of the resurrection as words of comfort for those in Thessalonica who have lost loved ones to death. "For the Lord Himself will descend from heaven with a shout, with the voice of the archangel and with the trumpet of God, and the dead in Christ will rise first. Then we who are alive and remain will be caught up together with them in the clouds to meet the Lord in the air, and so we shall always be with the Lord. Therefore comfort one another with these words" (1 Thessalonians 4:16–18).

This verse most likely gave rise to the idea of "the Rapture."

Our Part in the Last Day

I have my ideas on how the last day will unfold. It is just that—an idea. What I do know is that when Jesus returns, the day will happen just as He determines. My idea and your idea will not be factors. The events of the day will be under control of the King of Kings. "For this reason also, God highly exalted Him, and bestowed on Him the name which is above every name, so that at the name of Jesus every knee will bow, of those who are in heaven and on earth and under the earth, and that every tongue will confess that Jesus Christ is Lord, to the glory of God the Father" (Philippians 2:9–11).

Our part in the resurrection is to overcome the weakness of the flesh by giving our lives to the Lord and to be ready and waiting for the return of Jesus. In the Gospel of Mark, as Jesus returns from His prayer in the garden of Gethsemane, He finds His disciples asleep. He understands the weakness of the flesh because He is flesh Himself. Even so, in my mind, the words He speaks to them carry the sound of His disappointment. "And He came and found them sleeping, and said to Peter, 'Simon, are you asleep? Could you not keep watch for one hour? Keep watching and praying that you may not come into temptation; the spirit is willing, but the flesh is weak'" (Mark 14:37–38).

The return of Jesus for the resurrection day is as certain as His first appearance on earth. God has never failed to keep any of His promises. Jesus will return. The question is this: what will He find when He returns? "I tell you that He will bring about justice for them quickly. However, when the Son of Man comes, will He find faith on the earth?" (Luke 18:8).

Who will He find waiting? Me? You? Anyone? I do not want to be the one who disappoints the Savior. I pray you are there waiting with me.

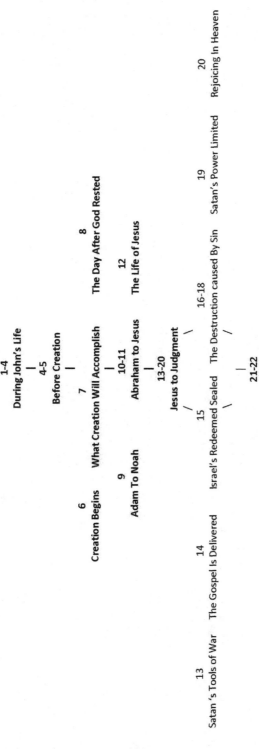

1-4
During John's Life

4-5
Before Creation

6
Creation Begins

7
What Creation Will Accomplish

8
The Day After God Rested

9
Adam To Noah

10-11
Abraham to Jesus

12
The Life of Jesus

13
Satan 's Tools of War

14
The Gospel Is Delivered

15
Israel's Redeemed Sealed

13-20
Jesus to Judgment

16-18
The Destruction caused By Sin

19
Satan's Power Limited

20
Rejoicing In Heaven

21-22
Judgment And a New World

Index

144,000 33, 54, 60, 61
666 58

A

Abyss 42, 48, 77, 88, 89
Adam xii, 9, 30, 31, 36, 37, 38, 42, 69
Adversary 30, 37, 41, 62, 74, 97
Alpha xii, 3, 8, 28, 97
Angel 3, 4, 9, 27, 32, 34, 36, 37, 42,
    44, 46, 53, 54, 61, 62, 63, 65,
    66, 67, 71, 73, 76, 77, 78, 81,
    83, 84, 85, 86, 87, 91, 95, 97
Angels 3, 4, 9, 27, 32, 34, 36, 37, 42,
    44, 46, 53, 54, 61, 62, 63, 65,
    66, 67, 71, 73, 76, 77, 78, 81,
    83, 84, 85, 86, 87, 91, 95, 97
Apostle 1, 4, 6, 7, 20, 22, 31, 61, 65,
    72, 89, 93, 94
Armageddon 69, 73
Authority 3, 8, 13, 16, 17, 21, 22, 28,
    30, 53, 54, 56, 65, 73, 77, 78,
    79, 80, 81, 85, 86, 87, 88, 89,
    91, 96, 97

B

Babylon 17, 30, 62, 63, 74, 76, 77, 79,
    80, 81, 82, 83, 84, 85
Baptism 6, 11
Beast 41, 48, 56, 57, 58, 59, 61, 62, 63,
    66, 70, 73, 76, 77, 78, 79, 80,
    87, 91
Birth 21, 23, 27, 49, 51, 52, 54, 77, 78

Bitter 37, 38, 46, 47
Blind 18, 22, 67
Blood 8, 18, 21, 27, 34, 38, 42, 48, 49,
    55, 60, 63, 65, 70, 71, 77, 86,
    90, 91, 98
Bottomless 41, 42
Bound 27, 30, 37, 88
Bowls 67, 69, 70, 71, 72, 73, 76
Bride 85, 86, 93, 94
Broken 26, 27, 28, 29, 30, 31, 35, 47,
    55, 95
Bronze 12, 24

C

Carrion 87
Censer 36
Chains 88
Church 1, 2, 3, 4, 5, 6, 7, 8, 9, 11, 12,
    13, 14, 15, 16, 17, 18, 19, 20,
    21, 22, 47, 55, 85, 86
Churches 2, 3, 4, 5, 6, 7, 9, 11, 14, 15,
    20, 21, 22
Congregation 4, 5, 6, 8, 15
Created 21, 24, 28, 33, 39, 44, 46, 58,
    59, 64, 68, 70, 79, 80, 97
Creation xii, 20, 21, 23, 24, 26, 28, 29,
    30, 31, 35, 36, 37, 39, 41, 42,
    43, 69, 70, 77, 89, 97
Crown 9, 22, 29, 53, 64, 65, 70

D

Danger 13, 33, 38, 39, 40

Darkness 38, 39, 42, 55, 68
David 16
Dead 1, 64, 74, 87, 89, 90, 99
Death 3, 8, 9, 13, 16, 20, 21, 29, 30,
    31, 36, 42, 50, 55, 57, 63, 64,
    66, 71, 73, 81, 84, 85, 89, 90,
    92, 94, 96, 97, 98, 99
Deeds 7, 10, 12, 15, 27, 72, 81, 85
Demons 51, 53, 54, 72, 81, 89
Devil 8, 9, 10, 30, 41, 42, 49, 53, 57,
    58, 59, 60, 63, 64, 71, 73, 77,
    78, 79, 83, 89, 91
Doom 37, 63, 64, 65, 66, 81
Door 9, 10, 16, 18, 21, 71, 72, 89
Dragon 30, 37, 52, 53, 54, 55, 56, 57,
    61, 62, 63, 64, 77, 87, 90

E

East 24, 41, 56, 72
Economy 6, 8, 12, 30
Egypt 45, 47, 50, 82
Elijah 49
Ephesus 6, 7, 8
Euphrates 72

F

Faith xi, 1, 5, 9, 10, 12, 13, 14, 16, 17,
    20, 31, 40, 44, 45, 48, 50, 54,
    58, 59, 61, 63, 64, 67, 80, 83,
    89, 95, 100
Faithful 10, 13, 16, 17, 54, 67, 86
Falsehood 2
Feast 18, 85, 87
Feet 2, 12, 16, 42, 46
Fellow Servant 86, 97
Fifth 31, 37, 39, 41, 62, 71
First xii, 3, 6, 7, 8, 9, 11, 12, 14, 29,
    30, 31, 32, 33, 36, 37, 39, 41,
    43, 44, 53, 56, 57, 58, 59, 62,
    70, 71, 73, 77, 80, 84, 88, 89,
    90, 92, 94, 97, 99, 100
First beast 56, 57, 58, 59, 73
Flesh 5, 8, 15, 21, 27, 42, 43, 55, 56,
    57, 59, 62, 63, 70, 71, 73, 74,

    75, 79, 82, 87, 100
Flood 40, 43, 44, 92
Flying 39, 61
Foretelling xi
Forty 8, 11, 47, 49, 54
Four 10, 22, 24, 34, 39, 44, 50, 54, 56,
    65, 71, 72, 79, 84, 85
Fourth 30, 31, 37, 38, 39, 71
Future xi, xii, 4, 16, 20, 34, 76

G

Gates 94, 95
Glass 22, 23, 66, 68, 73
Gold 3, 14, 18, 22, 67, 72
Golden 14, 29, 36, 47, 64, 77, 89
Gospel xi, 1, 3, 11, 15, 46, 51, 60, 61,
    62, 63, 64, 65, 66, 67, 70, 71,
    73, 78, 79, 82, 84, 87, 88, 89,
    97, 98, 100

H

Hallelujah 84, 85
Harlot 76, 77, 78, 79, 80, 81, 82, 83,
    85
Harvest 60, 65
Heaven 2, 3, 4, 8, 11, 15, 16, 18, 21,
    22, 23, 24, 26, 27, 28, 30, 32,
    33, 35, 37, 41, 43, 50, 51, 52,
    53, 54, 57, 60, 61, 63, 66, 71,
    77, 79, 82, 84, 85, 86, 89, 91,
    92, 93, 96, 97, 99, 100
Hebrew 11, 23, 24, 31, 45, 49, 50, 62,
    63, 64, 67, 72, 74, 86
History xii, 2, 9, 16, 20, 31, 32, 43, 44,
    49, 55, 58, 76
Holy 9, 16, 24, 47, 62, 68, 78, 82, 85,
    91
Honor xi, 24, 25, 28, 47, 67
Horns 56, 77, 79
Horseman 29, 30, 31, 37, 43
Horses 29, 30, 41, 44, 86, 89
Hundred 43, 50, 54

I

Israel 22, 33, 40, 44, 48, 49, 50, 52, 54, 60, 61, 63, 94, 95
Israelites xii, 24, 36, 40, 55

J

Jews 5, 6, 8, 16, 32, 50, 61, 88, 94

K

Key 42
Kingdom 10, 13, 14, 16, 21, 27, 51, 72, 83, 89
King of Kings 53, 87, 100
Kings xi, 6, 11, 12, 22, 24, 30, 52, 53, 62, 63, 72, 76, 78, 79, 87, 91, 100

L

Lamb 25, 27, 28, 33, 34, 35, 55, 58, 60, 67, 73, 79, 84, 85, 91, 96, 98
Lament 82
Lamp 22, 23
Lampstand 2, 3, 4, 49
Laodicea 15, 17, 18
Lie 1, 2, 17, 18, 31, 42, 57, 58, 60, 61, 64, 73, 77, 78, 79, 87, 88, 89
Light 3, 7, 22, 23, 26, 27, 36, 38, 39, 49, 67, 68, 71, 84, 95, 96
Lightning 20, 22, 23, 36
Listen vii, 7, 9, 11, 13, 15, 17, 18, 19, 50, 61, 89
Little book 46, 47, 49, 60
Locusts 41, 44
Love 3, 7, 8, 9, 11, 12, 18, 24, 27, 32, 34, 43, 51, 57, 58, 61, 62, 63, 73, 74, 79, 82, 85, 86, 87, 89, 92, 96
Lukewarm 18
Lust 57, 59, 73, 74, 76, 79, 80, 82, 87

M

Mark of the Beast 56, 58, 70
Marriage v, 84, 85, 86

Martyrs 31
Measure 30, 48, 95
Message vii, xii, 1, 2, 3, 5, 6, 7, 8, 9, 10, 11, 12, 13, 14, 15, 17, 18, 19, 20, 46, 61, 62, 66, 67, 72, 73, 74, 75, 77, 78, 79, 82, 86, 88, 89, 94, 98
Michael 4
Millstone 83
Moses xi, xii, 47, 48, 49, 50, 51, 55, 59, 61, 64, 67, 73, 82
Multitude 33, 36, 71, 84, 85
Mystery 26, 27, 46, 47, 56, 77

N

Naked 18, 38
Nebuchadnezzar 62, 63
New Earth 93
New Heaven 93, 97
New Song 26, 27
Nicolaitans 7, 10, 11
Noah 39, 40, 43, 44, 55
North 24, 56

O

Olive 49, 95
Omega xii, 3, 8, 28, 97
Outer court 48, 49

P

Pause 32
Pergamum 8, 9, 10
Persecute 76
Persecuted 12, 31, 64, 83
Philadelphia 15, 16, 19
Plagues 44, 66, 67, 68, 69, 70, 71, 72, 73, 74
Plan 21, 26, 27, 28, 29, 31, 32, 33, 35, 36, 37, 44, 46, 48, 49, 50, 51, 53, 55, 67, 68, 71, 80, 81, 84, 88, 91, 97
Praise 7, 10, 15, 23, 24, 26, 28, 36, 71, 73, 84, 85
Prediction xi, xii, 20

Promise 8, 9, 13, 16, 17, 20, 33, 36, 45, 46, 47, 49, 57, 63, 64, 72, 77, 90, 94, 95, 96, 97, 100
Prophecy xi, xii, 50, 53, 54, 97

R

Rain 48, 49
Rapture 99
Reapers 60, 64, 65
Redemption 36, 64, 67, 97
Repent 7, 10, 11, 13, 15, 18, 44, 68, 71, 72, 78, 84
Repented 7, 40
Resurrection 1, 3, 20, 53, 54, 63, 71, 79, 88, 90, 99, 100
Revelation vii, xi, xii, 1, 2, 3, 5, 6, 8, 9, 11, 12, 14, 15, 17, 20, 21, 22, 23, 24, 26, 27, 29, 30, 31, 33, 35, 36, 37, 38, 39, 41, 43, 44, 46, 47, 48, 49, 51, 52, 53, 54, 55, 56, 57, 58, 60, 61, 62, 63, 64, 65, 66, 67, 69, 70, 71, 72, 73, 76, 77, 78, 79, 80, 81, 82, 83, 84, 85, 86, 87, 88, 90, 91, 93, 94, 95, 96, 97, 98
River of Life 96
Rod of Iron 53
Rome xii, 6, 54

S

Sacrifice 18, 24, 33, 62, 71, 74, 86
Saints 8, 9, 10, 12, 16, 36, 47, 51, 68, 77, 78, 79, 83, 84, 85, 86, 91, 99
Salvation vii, 7, 19, 21, 29, 31, 32, 33, 34, 36, 39, 40, 43, 44, 45, 48, 51, 60, 61, 62, 71, 72, 73, 74, 75, 78, 84, 88, 89, 92, 95, 97
Sardis 14, 15
Satan 1, 4, 8, 10, 16, 30, 31, 37, 41, 42, 43, 44, 50, 51, 53, 54, 55, 56, 57, 59, 63, 70, 71, 72, 73, 77, 78, 79, 87, 88, 89, 90, 91, 92
Scripture iv, vii, 22, 27, 30, 49, 50, 67, 70, 72

Scroll 25, 26, 27, 28, 29, 32, 33, 35, 36, 44
Sea 3, 20, 22, 23, 24, 37, 38, 55, 56, 57, 66, 67, 68, 70, 73, 77, 83
Seal 26, 27, 28, 29, 30, 31, 32, 35, 37, 41, 55, 60
Second 6, 9, 30, 33, 37, 38, 50, 54, 57, 58, 59, 61, 62, 65, 70, 73, 84, 90, 91, 92
Second beast 57, 58, 59, 61, 73
Servant vii, 10, 15, 32, 62, 67, 86, 97
Seven 2, 3, 5, 6, 20, 21, 22, 23, 26, 36, 46, 49, 53, 56, 58, 66, 67, 76, 77, 78
Seventh 32, 35, 48, 62, 73, 76
Sickle 64, 65
Silence 35, 89
Sin 10, 13, 15, 18, 21, 30, 31, 32, 37, 38, 39, 40, 59, 62, 63, 64, 67, 69, 71, 73, 74, 76, 78, 82, 85, 87, 89, 90, 91, 92, 93, 96
Sixth 31, 32, 44, 46, 72, 78
Slain 25, 27, 28, 31, 50, 58, 79
Smyrna 8, 9
Song 26, 27, 60, 67
South 24, 56
Spirit 7, 9, 15, 21, 22, 23, 24, 27, 30, 36, 51, 56, 58, 62, 64, 73, 74, 75, 79, 81, 86, 87, 89, 100
Spiritual 14, 22, 27, 39, 42, 55, 56, 82, 87
Stars 2, 3, 4, 13, 37, 41, 52, 77, 94
Stomach 47
Sun xii, 46, 67, 71
Sword 2, 10, 11, 31, 64, 87
Synagogue 6, 8, 16

T

Temple 6, 15, 17, 24, 36, 48, 49, 54, 65, 67, 95
Temptations 5, 17, 30, 42, 57, 59, 66, 82, 84, 100
Ten 8, 24, 56, 77, 79
Terror 31, 43, 70, 73

Testimony 16, 49, 55, 61, 67, 86, 90
Third 30, 35, 37, 38, 41, 43, 53, 63, 70, 77, 85, 92
Thousand 23, 24, 30, 54, 88, 89, 90, 99
Three 6, 7, 9, 23, 24, 30, 35, 39, 40, 43, 44, 50, 54, 73, 74, 98
Throne 6, 10, 16, 20, 21, 22, 23, 24, 25, 28, 46, 48, 51, 67, 69, 71, 85, 90, 91, 96, 97
Thunder 20, 22, 23, 36, 46, 47, 74
Thyatira 11, 12, 13
Time vii, xii, 3, 6, 8, 10, 11, 13, 14, 15, 17, 18, 20, 21, 22, 23, 27, 30, 33, 39, 40, 41, 47, 49, 53, 61, 64, 65, 66, 70, 71, 72, 77, 78, 79, 82, 84, 88, 89, 90, 91, 96, 97, 98
Tree of life 7, 29, 96
Tribulation 7, 8, 9, 16, 33
Trumpet 2, 35, 36, 37, 38, 39, 40, 41, 44, 46, 48, 51, 52, 55, 71, 99
Truth vii, 2, 7, 10, 11, 16, 17, 21, 39, 57, 58, 60, 61, 62, 70, 71, 74, 78, 87, 88, 89, 90
Twelve 22, 24, 33, 61, 94
Twenty-four 22, 34, 85

V

Vision vii, xii, 1, 2, 3, 4, 8, 18, 20, 21, 23, 24, 25, 27, 30, 32, 33, 34, 35, 37, 39, 41, 43, 44, 49, 52, 54, 55, 56, 60, 61, 67, 73, 76, 77, 79, 82, 86, 87, 97, 98, 99
Voice 2, 3, 6, 16, 30, 37, 50, 51, 54, 63, 73, 82, 85, 89, 99

W

War 4, 30, 42, 48, 52, 54, 56, 60, 61, 73, 77, 79, 80, 90, 91
Water 2, 6, 37, 38, 43, 48, 49, 56, 69, 70, 71, 76, 80, 85, 96
Wealth 6, 11, 14, 15, 18, 57, 74, 77, 81, 82
Wedding 85, 94
West 24, 56
Witnesses 48, 49, 50
Woe 35, 39, 40, 41, 43, 44, 50, 54, 92
Woman 11, 12, 13, 30, 36, 52, 53, 54, 61, 63, 76, 77, 90
Wormwood 37, 38
Worship 5, 6, 12, 18, 21, 23, 24, 25, 34, 36, 44, 48, 58, 59, 63, 72, 76, 78, 79, 86, 94, 95, 97
Wrath 31, 36, 54, 66, 67, 69, 71, 73, 74, 75, 78, 79, 82

Y

Year v, 6, 11, 23, 30, 43, 45, 47, 50, 53, 62, 67, 88, 89, 90, 99

Z

Zion 60

Printed in the United States
by Baker & Taylor Publisher Services